Baby Booties and Slippers

Baby Booties and Slippers

30 designs to stitch, knit and crochet

Susie Johns

*For my children Josh, Lillie and Edith, who are a constant support
and inspiration, bless their tiny little toes...*

First published 2013 by
Guild of Master Craftsman Publications Ltd
Castle Place, 166 High Street, Lewes,
East Sussex BN7 1XU

ISBN 978-1-86108-960-1

Publisher Jonathan Bailey
Production Manager Jim Bulley
Managing Editor Gerrie Purcell
Senior Project Editor Virginia Brehaut
Copy Editor Nicola Hodgson
Managing Art Editor Gilda Pacitti
Designer Ali Walper
Photographer Sian Irvine

Set in Kozuka and Aji Hand
Colour origination by GMC Reprographics
Printed and bound in China

Contents

Introduction 8

The Projects

1 Heart felt 10

2 Rabbit ears 14

3 Cowboy boots 18

4 Rainbow patchwork 22

5 Daisy Jane 26

6 Simple shoes 30

7 Gingham check 34

8 Elfin boots 38

9 Little duckling 42

10 Cosy slippers 46

11 Princess jewels 50

12 Lacy sandals 54

13 Ballet slippers 58

14 Puppy dog 62

15 Strappy sandals 66

16 Crossover pumps 70

17 Seaside stripes 74

18 Watermelon slices 78

19 Button boots 82

20 Baseball boots 86

21 Frog face 90

22 Ladybird slippers 94

23 Inuit boots 98

24 Jungle print 102

25 Winter warmers 106

26 Fresh blossom 110

27 Ankle tie 114

28 Stripy booties 118

29 Teddy bear 122

30 Colourful cupcakes 126

Techniques

Sewing techniques 132

Knitting techniques 138

Crochet techniques 146

Add-on soles 152

Size chart 154

Abbreviations 156

Conversions 157

About the author 158

Acknowledgements 158

Index 159

Introduction

Keeping your baby's toes cosy and warm is important – and it has never been such fun! Whether you like to sew, knit or crochet – or maybe, like me, all three – you will find many patterns to please within these pages.

Many people take up their needles or hooks for the first time when there is a baby on the way. If you are a novice, making tiny baby garments is a great way to learn a new craft – and baby slippers and booties, being particularly tiny, are relatively quick to make.

If you are new to knitting, you could begin with the Crossover Pumps on page 70; if you are a crochet novice, the Simple Shoes on page 30 are a good place to start; and if you can manage only the most basic sewing projects, try the Heart Felt on page 10, as they are so simple to stitch.

The projects in this book are not all designed for beginners, however; there are plenty of interesting techniques to keep the seasoned needlecrafter satisfied. These projects might be small but there is plenty of scope for creativity when making them.

My own three children, now grown up and definitely 'too big for their boots', wore hand-made slippers and booties when they were babies, and as all three of them are now pretty handy with a sewing needle or a crochet hook, I expect they will make similar little items for their own babies, when the time comes.

I had such fun creating these cute shoes, and I hope you have as much enjoyment in making them.

Safety Note One important thing to note: these are baby booties and slippers. They are meant to be worn in the pram, when crawling around on the floor, or snuggling on the sofa for a bedtime story – they are not designed for walking. The addition of non-slip soles, as described on page 152, will add a bit of grip on slippers for older babies who are starting to find their feet but will not make them safe for walking. Always use your common sense.

Heart felt

Little toes will be ultra-cosy in slippers made from felted wool. Show how much you care by stitching an appliqué heart on the front of each one.

Size

To fit sizes 0–3[3–6:6–9:9–12] months
See size guide on pages 154–5

Pattern note

Seam allowances are ¼in (6mm) unless otherwise stated.

Pattern pieces

You will need the following pattern pieces from the pull-out sheet.

1 Left sole · cut 1 in blue felt
2 Right sole · cut 1 in blue felt
3 Upper · cut 2 in blue felt
4 Heart appliqué · cut 2 in red felt

Materials and equipment

- Piece of wool felt or wool-viscose felt, approximately 15¾ x 12in (40 x 30cm), in pale blue
- Small scrap of wool felt or wool-viscose felt, in red
- Sewing needle
- Crewel needle
- 6-stranded embroidery thread, in red
- Sewing thread, in colours to match felt
- Sewing machine (optional)

1 Trace the pattern pieces listed on page 10 from the pull-out sheet on to tracing paper and cut out to make templates (see page 134). Use the templates to cut two soles and two uppers from pale blue felt and two heart motifs from red. Place one heart motif on each upper, positioning the top of the heart just below the slit at centre front. Pin, then stitch firmly in place, oversewing the edges of the motif.

2 Place the two short straight edges of the upper together and stitch to form back seam (seam is on inside of shoe). To keep seam allowance on the back seam flat, press seam open and topstitch on either side of the seam.

3 Pin the sole to the upper with the seam allowance on the outside of each shoe. Stitch sole to upper. Using three strands of red embroidery thread, work blanket stitch (see page 136) all round the edge of each shoe, inserting the needle through both thicknesses of fabric.

♥ ♥ ♥   Both wool felt and wool-viscose felt are practical and hard-wearing choices for baby and toddler slippers (do not use craft felt). Once made, the slippers can be dry-cleaned. If you would prefer to have washable slippers, you should wash the fabric before cutting and stitching the shoes, to pre-shrink it. This means that it shouldn't shrink again once the slippers are made. It may, however, alter the texture of the fabric, creating a dimpled appearance. ♥ ♥ ♥

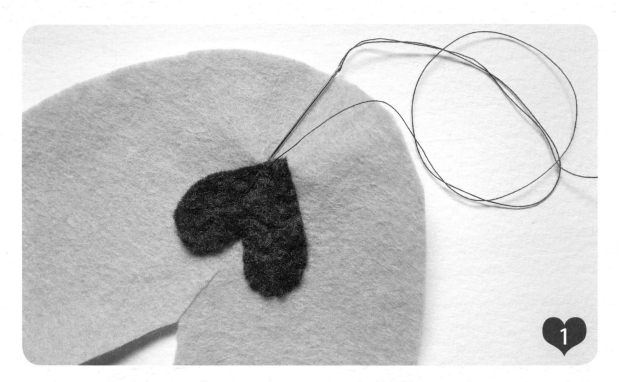

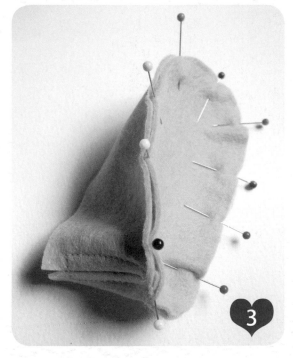

Rabbit ears

Cosy and cute, these bunny booties are full of character and will amuse your baby as well as keeping tiny toes really snug on a cold day.

Size

To fit sizes 0–3[3–6:6–9] months
See size guide on pages 154–5

Tension

22 sts and 40 rows to 4in (10cm), measured over garter stitch, using 3.25mm needles. Use larger or smaller needles if necessary to obtain correct tension.

Materials and equipment

- 1 x 50g ball Artesano Superwash Merino DK yarn in shade 0157 White (A)
- 1 x 50g ball Artesano Superwash Merino DK yarn in shade 0043 Baby Pink (B)
- 1 pair of 3.25mm (UK10:US3) needles
- 2 stitch holders or safety pins
- Tapestry needle
- 4 sew-on googly eyes
- Sewing needle and white thread

Main piece (make 2)

Using yarn A, cast on 25[29:33] sts.
Knit 24[28:32] rows.

Next row: K16[19:22], turn and leave rem sts on a holder.

Next row: K7[9:11], placing a stitch marker in the last st worked, then turn and leave rem sts on a holder.

Knit 20[24:28] rows for instep.

Next row: K2tog, k to last 2 sts, k2tog (5[7:9] sts).

Knit 1 row.

Leaving sts on needle, cut yarn and rejoin to marked stitch, then pick up and knit 10[12:14] sts up edge of instep, k5[7:9] sts from needle, 10[12:14] sts down opposite edge of instep and 9[10:11] sts from stitch holder (34[41:48] sts).

Next row: K34[41:48], then knit 9[10:11] sts from other stitch holder (43[51:59] sts).

Knit 6[8:10] rows.

SHAPE SOLE

Row 1: K24[28:32], k2tog tbl, turn and leave rem 17[21:25] sts on left-hand needle.

Row 2: K6, k2tog, turn and leave rem 17[21:25] sts on left-hand needle.

♥ ♥ ♥ **Instead of googly eyes, which could be a choking hazard if they are not securely stitched to the knitted fabric, you could embroider the eyes using black yarn.** ♥ ♥ ♥

Row 3: K6, k2tog tbl, turn and leave rem 16[20:24] sts on needle.

Row 4: K6, k2tog, turn and leave rem 16[20:24] sts on needle.

Continue in this way, until you have worked the row: k6, k2tog tbl, turn and leave rem 5[5:7] sts on needle, then k6, k2tog, k5[5:7]; cast off.

Ear (make 4)

Using yarn A, cast on 6 sts.

Row 1 (and each odd-numbered row): Knit.

Row 2: K1, inc1, k2, inc1, k1 (8 sts).

Row 4: K1, inc1, k4, inc1, k1 (10 sts).

Row 6: K1, inc1, k6, inc1, k1 (12 sts).

Row 8: K1, inc1, k8, inc1, k1 (14 sts).

Row 10: K1, sl1, k1, psso, k8, k2tog, k1 (12 sts).

Row 12: K1, sl1, k1, psso, k6, k2tog, k1 (10 sts).

Row 14: K1, sl1, k1, psso, k4, k2tog, k1 (8 sts).

Row 16: K1, sl1, k1, psso, k2, k2tog, k1 (6 sts).

Row 18: K1, sl1, k1, psso, k2tog, k1 (4 sts).

Row 20: K1, sl1, k2tog, psso (2 sts).

Row 21: K2tog; cut yarn and fasten off.

Ear lining (make 4)

Using yarn B, cast on 5 sts.

Row 1 (and each odd-numbered row): Purl.

Row 2: K1, inc1, k1, inc1, k1 (7 sts).

Row 4: K1, inc1, k3, inc1, k1 (9 sts).

Row 6: K1, inc1, k5, inc1, k1 (11 sts).

Row 8: K1, inc1, k7, inc1, k1 (13 sts).

Row 10: K1, sl1, k1, psso, k7, k2tog, k1 (11 sts).

Row 12: K1, sl1, k1, psso, k5, k2tog, k1 (9 sts).

Row 14: K1, sl1, k1, psso, k3, k2tog, k1 (7 sts).

Row 16: K1, sl1, k1, psso, k1, k2tog, k1 (5 sts).

Row 18: K1, sl1, k2tog, psso, k1 (3 sts).

Row 19: P3tog; cut yarn and fasten off.

Making up

With right sides together, stitch back seam, including heel, and fold top of leg to right side to form a cuff. Pair ears with ear linings and stitch lining to ear, then stitch two ears to each bootie at base of leg, taking a few stitches through the inner edge of the ear and the leg of the bootie. Thread tapestry needle with a length of yarn B and embroider a nose in satin stitch (see page 135) on the centre front of each bootie. Stitch googly eyes firmly and securely in place with white thread. With yarn A, make a 1¼in (3cm) pompom for each bootie and sew to back seam.

💜 🖤 💜 Even without the bunny ears, these booties are a lovely shape and relatively easy and quick to make, knitted in one piece with only the back seam to stitch – so why not make them in a plain colour? One pair in any of the three sizes uses less than a single 50g ball of yarn. 💜 🖤 💜

Cowboy boots

Wild West-style booties are just the thing for a tiny tenderfoot. Here they are made in a stylish combination of grey-green and cream, although you could choose any two contrasting colours.

Size
To fit sizes 6–12[12–15:15–18] months
See size guide on pages 154–5

Tension
19 sts and 22 rows to 4in (10cm), measured over rows of double crochet, using 3.50mm hook. Use a larger or smaller hook if necessary to obtain correct tension.

Materials and equipment
• 1 x 50g ball Debbie Bliss Bella yarn in shade 16004 Ecru (A)
• 1 x 50g ball Debbie Bliss Bella yarn in shade 16015 Sea Green (B)
• 3.50mm (UK9:USE-4) crochet hook
• Tapestry needle

Bootie (make 2)

Foundation chain: Using yarn A, make 36[40:44]ch.

Foundation row (RS): 1dc in 2nd ch from hook, 1dc in each ch to end (35[39:43] sts).

Row 1: 1ch, 1dc in 1st dc, 1dc in each dc to end; cut A and join in B on last st. Using B, rep row 1 a further 6[8:10] times.

Next row: 1ch, 1dc in 1st dc, 1dc in each of next 2dc, (dc2tog over next 2dc, 1dc in each of next 2dc) 8 [9:10] times (27[30:33] sts).

Next row: 1ch, 1dc in each st. Rep last row twice more.

Next row: 1ch, 1dc in each of first 3 dc, (2dc in next dc, 1dc in each of next 2dc) 8[9:10] times (35[39:43] sts).

Next row: 1ch, 1dc in each st; fasten off and place marker in last st; turn.

INSTEP

With RS facing, miss first 12[13:14]dc and join yarn A to next dc.

Row 1: 1ch, 1dc in 1st dc, 1dc in each of next 10[12:14]dc; turn.

Row 2: 1ch, 1dc in each of these centre 11[13:15]dc, inserting hook into front loop only.

Row 3: 1ch, 1dc in each dc of previous row. Rep row 3 a further 5[7:9] times.

Next row: 1ch, dc2tog over next dc, 1dc in next 7[9:11]dc, dc2tog over next 2 sts (9[11:13] sts).

Next row: 1ch, 1dc in each dc to end.

Next row: 1ch, dc2tog over next dc, 1dc in next 5[7:9]dc, dc2tog over next 2 sts (7[9:11] sts).

Next row: 1ch, 1dc in each dc to end; fasten off.

With RS facing, rejoin yarn to marked st and work 1ch, 1dc in each of next 12[13:14]dc, 8[10:12]dc evenly spaced up side of instep, 1dc in each dc along top edge, 8[10:12]dc down other side of instep and 1dc in each dc to end of row (47[55:63] sts).

Row 2: 1ch, 1dc in each dc of previous row. Rep row 2 a further 4[6:8] times; cut A and join in B on last st.

SOLE

Row 1: Using yarn B, 1ch, 1dc in each of next 21[25:29]dc, dc2tog over next 2dc, 1dc in next dc, dc2tog over next 2dc, 1dc in each of next 21[25:29]dc (45[53:61] sts).

Row 2: 1ch, 1dc in 1st dc, (dc2tog over next 2dc, 1dc in each of next 17[21:25] dc, dc2tog over next 2dc, 1dc in next dc) twice (41[49:57] sts).

Row 3: 1ch, 1dc in 1st dc, (dc2tog over next 2dc, 1dc in each of next 15[19:23] dc, dc2tog over next 2dc, 1dc in next dc) twice (37[45:53] sts).

Row 4: 1ch, 1dc in 1st dc, (dc2tog over next 2dc, 1dc in each of next 13[17:21] dc, dc2tog over next 2dc, 1dc in next dc) twice (33[41:49] sts).

♥ ❤ ♥ The cotton-rich yarn used to make these booties gives a firm result, helping them to hold their shape, but it also includes a touch of silk and cashmere for softness. You could make them in a different cotton blend: just make sure that the tension matches that stated in the pattern instructions. ♥ ❤ ♥

Row 5: 1ch, 1dc in 1st dc, (dc2tog over next 2dc, 1dc in each of next 11[15:19] dc, dc2tog over next 2dc, 1dc in next dc) twice; cut yarn and fasten off.

TONGUE
With RS facing and toe towards you, return to row 2 of the upper and the unworked back loops, which are on the RS of the work.
Miss the first 3 loops and rejoin yarn A to next loop.
Row 1: 1ch, 1dc in 1st loop, 1dc in each of next 4[6:8] loops; turn (5[7:9] sts).
Row 2: 1ch, 1dc in each dc of previous row.
Rep row 2 a further 3[5:7] times.
Next row: 1ch, 2dc in 1st st, 1dc in each dc to last st, 2dc in last dc; turn (7[9:11] sts).
Next row: 1ch, 1dc in each of first 1[2:3]dc, 1htr in next st, 1tr in next st, 1dtr in next st, 1tr in next st, 1htr in next st, 1dc in each st to end of row; fasten off.
Repeat for other bootie.

Loop
Using yarn A, make 4ch.
Foundation row (RS): 1dc in 2nd ch from hook, 1dc in each ch to end (3 sts).

Row 1: 1ch, 1dc in 1st dc, 1dc in each dc to end.
Rep row 1 a further 10 times.
Cut yarn and fasten off.

Making up
Stitch underfoot and back seams. Stitch the tongue firmly to the front of the bootie by oversewing the edges, stitch by stitch, using the tail of yarn; then stitch the two ends of the loop to the top of the bootie, over the back seam.

Rainbow patchwork

These little shoes can be as colourful as you like. They are a great way of using up even the tiniest fabric scraps from your workbasket.

Size

To fit sizes 0–3[3–6:6–9:9–12] months
See size guide on pages 154–5

Pattern note

Seam allowances are 1/4in (6mm) unless otherwise stated.

Pattern pieces

You will need the following pattern pieces from the pull-out sheet.

5 Upper • cut 2 in patchwork and 2 in lining fabric

6 Sole • cut 2 in chosen sole fabric and 2 in lining

Materials and equipment

- Scraps of 100% cotton dress-weight fabric, in various prints
- Piece of 100% cotton dress-weight fabric, approximately 15 3/4 x 12in (40 x 30cm), in orange and white gingham check, for lining
- Piece of 100% cotton dress-weight fabric, approximately 6 x 4in (15 x 10cm), for base of sole
- Sewing needle
- Sewing thread, in colour to match fabric
- 60in (150cm) of 1in (25mm) bias binding
- Sewing machine (optional)

1 Choose nine cotton fabrics of similar weight, selecting as many different colours and patterns as possible. Cut nine strips of fabric, all different, each measuring 4³/₄ x 2¹/₂in (12 x 6cm).

2 Stitch the fabric strips together along their long sides, to make three pieces of three strips each. Press each piece, pressing the seam allowances to one side, then cut each piece in half across the centre of the strips.

3 Divide the six pieces into two batches and stitch together, to make two nine-patch pieces that are mirror images of each other. Press each piece, pressing the seam allowances to one side. Trace the pattern pieces listed on page 22 from the pull-out sheet on to tracing paper and cut out to make templates (see page 134). Use the templates to cut two uppers each from the patchwork and the lining material, and two soles from the lining and a contrast fabric.

4 Pin, then stitch the back seam on each patchwork upper, then do the same with the two uppers in the lining fabric. Press seams flat. Pair up each upper with its lining, with right sides out; pin, then baste together close to edges. Do the same with the soles, then pin the sole to the upper on each shoe, with the seam allowance on the outside, and baste.

5 Stitch upper to sole, by hand or machine, then use bias binding to bind the front edge of the upper, leaving the ends open to form a casing, and insert a length of cord elastic into each casing, stitching the ends of the elastic to the fabric of the shoe at either end.

6 Now bind the back edge of each shoe, with an extra 8–10in (20–25cm) of extra binding at each side to form ties. Finally, bind all around the base, starting and ending at centre back of sole and covering the seam allowance.

♥ ♥ ♥ **Cotton fabric is the best choice for these patchwork shoes; it is readily available in a wide range of colours and prints and can be bought in small quantities. Some cotton fabrics are pre-shrunk, but it is a good idea when making patchwork to wash all fabrics first in case they shrink.** ♥ ♥ ♥

Daisy Jane

*Made in peppermint green and candy pink,
these slippers are simple to make and will
appeal to little girls who like dressing up.*

Size

To fit sizes 15–18[18–24:24–36] months
See size guide on pages 154–5

Tension

18 sts and 10 rows to 4in (10cm),
measured over rows of double crochet,
using a 4.00mm hook. Use a larger or
smaller hook if necessary to obtain
correct tension.

Pattern pieces

You will need the following pattern
pieces from the pull-out sheet.
7 Sole · cut 2 in soft leather

Materials and equipment

- 1 x 50g ball Rowan Belle Organic by
  Amy Butler DK yarn in shade 25 Dew (A)
- 1 x 50g ball Rowan Belle Organic by Amy
  Butler DK yarn in shade 29 Dahlia (B)
- 4.00mm (UK8:USG-6) crochet hook
- Piece of soft leather approximately
  7 x 7in (18 x 18cm)
- Leather punch
- Tapestry needle
- 4 small ball buttons, translucent
- Sewing needle and thread

Sole (make 2)

Trace the pattern pieces listed on page 26 from the pull-out sheet on to tracing paper and cut out to make templates (see page 134). Cut two soles from soft leather and punch 31[35:39] holes, as indicated on the pattern pieces.

Foundation round: Using yarn A, join yarn to hole at centre back of sole and work 1ch (does not count as st), 1dc in same place, then *1dc in next hole, 2dc in next hole; rep from * to end; join with sl st to 1st dc and fasten off (46[52:58] sts).

Upper (make 2)

Foundation chain: Using yarn A, make 30[36:42]ch; join with sl st to 1st ch to make a ring.

Round 1: 1ch (does not count as st), 1dc in 1st ch, 1dc in each of next 11[14:17] ch, 2dc in each of next 2ch, 1dc in each of next 2ch, 2dc in each of next 2ch, 1dc in each of next 12[15:18]ch, sl st in 1st dc (34[40:46] sts).

Round 2: 1ch, 1dc in 1st dc, 1dc in each of next 13[16:19]dc, 2dc in each of next 2 dc, 1dc in each of next 2dc, 2dc in each of next 2dc, 1dc in each of next 14[17:20]dc, sl st in 1st dc (38[44:50] sts).

Round 3: 1ch, 1dc in 1st st, 2dc in next st, 1dc in each of next 12[15:18] sts, (2dc in next st, 1dc in next st) twice, 2dc in each

of next 2 sts, (1dc in next st, 2dc in next st) twice, 1dc in each of next 12[15:18] sts, 2dc in next st, 1dc in last st; join with sl st to 1st dc of round (46[52:58] sts).

Work 2[3:4] rounds of dc without further shaping; fasten off but do not cut yarn.

Daisy (make 2)

Using yarn B, make 6ch and join with a sl st to 1st ch to make a ring.

Round 1: 1ch (does not count as st), 10dc in ring; join with sl st to 1st dc of round (10 sts).

Round 2: (6ch, sl st into next dc) 10 times; cut yarn, leaving a tail, and fasten off.

Flower centre (make 2)

Using yarn A, make a magic loop and work 1ch (does not count as st), 6dc into ring; join with a sl st to 1st dc and pull up tail of yarn to close gap in centre.
Round 1: 1ch (does not count as st), 2dc in each dc of 1st round; join with a sl st to 1st dc; cut yarn, leaving a tail, and fasten off (20 sts).

Strap (make 2)

Using yarn B, make 15[16:17]ch.
Row 1: 1dc in 6th ch, 1dc in each ch to end.
Cut yarn leaving a tail and fasten off.

Making up

To join the sole and upper, with wrong sides together and beginning at centre back, using yarn B, work 1sl st in each pair of stitches around perimeter, inserting the hook into the back loops only (one loop from upper and one loop from sole); cut yarn and fasten off. On the top edge of each shoe, beginning at centre back, using yarn B, work 1sl st in each stitch, inserting the hook into one loop only on foundation chain; cut yarn and fasten off.

Stitch end of strap to outside of shoe, halfway along side, making sure that the straps are on different sides to create a left and right shoe. Stitch a ball button on the opposite side of each shoe and fasten using the chain loop at the other end of each strap.

For the flower centre, thread the tail of yarn into a tapestry needle and thread through each loop around the edge, then pull up to gather and form a neat ball shape; stitch one flower centre to the centre of each daisy, then stitch one daisy firmly to the front of each shoe. Stitch a ball button to the centre of each, pulling the shank down inside the hole in the flower centre and fasten off securely.

Simple shoes

Quick and easy to crochet, these simple and pretty pram shoes can be made to match any special outfit or occasion.

Size

To fit sizes 0–3 [3–6:6–9:9–15] months
See size guide on pages 154–5

Tension

20 sts and 22 rows to 4in (10cm), measured over rows of double crochet, using 4.00mm hook. Use a larger or smaller hook if necessary to obtain correct tension.

Materials and equipment

• 1 x 50g ball Artesano Superwash Merino DK yarn in shade 5769 Baby Lavender
• 4.00mm (UK8:USG-6) crochet hook
• Tapestry needle
• 2 sets of snap fasteners

Sole (make 2)

Foundation chain: Make 9[11:13:15]ch.

Round 1: 1dc in 2nd ch from hook, 2dc in next ch, 1dc in next ch, 1htr in each of next 2[3:4:5] ch, 1tr in each of next 2[3:4:5] ch, 7tr in last ch; do not turn but work back along opposite side of foundation chain as follows: 1tr in each of next 2[3:4:5]ch, 1htr in each of next 2[3:4:5] ch, 1dc in next ch, 2dc in next ch, 1dc in next ch, join with sl st in 1st dc of round (23[27:31:35] sts).

Round 2: 3ch (counts as 1tr), 2tr in each of next 3 sts, 1tr in each of next 5[7:9:11] sts, 2tr in each of next 3 sts, 3tr in next st, 2tr in each of next 3 sts, 1tr in each of next 5[7:9:11] sts, 2tr in each of next 3 sts, join with sl st to 3rd of 3ch at beg of round (38[42:46:50] sts).

Cut yarn and fasten off.

Upper (make 2)

Foundation chain: Make 26[30:34:38]ch; join with sl st to 1st ch to make a ring.

Round 1: 1ch (does not count as st), 1dc in 1st ch, 1dc in each of next 9[11:13:15] ch, 2dc in each of next 2ch, 1dc in each of next 2ch, 2dc in each of next 2ch, 1dc in each of next 10[12:14:16]ch, sl st in 1st dc (30[34:38:42] sts).

Round 2: 1ch, 1dc in 1st st, 2dc in next st, 1dc in each of next 8[10:12:14] sts, (2dc in next st, 1dc in next st) twice, 2dc in each of next 2 sts, (1dc in next st, 2dc in next st) twice, 1dc in each of next 8[10:12:14] sts, 2dc in next st, 1dc in last st; join with sl st to 1st dc of round (38[42:46:50] sts). Work 3[4:5:6] rounds of dc without further shaping; fasten off but do not cut yarn.

Making up

To join sole and upper, with wrong sides together, work 1ch into same place as last st on upper and join with sl st to last st worked on sole, then continue by working 1sl st in each pair of stitches around perimeter; cut yarn and fasten off.

STRAP OF LEFT SHOE

Starting at centre back, count 5[6:7:8] sts to the right of this point along top edge of shoe and mark this stitch.

Foundation row: Make 24[27:30:33]ch, then work 1dc into marked st and 1dc into each of next 9[11:13:15] sts along top edge; turn.

Row 1: 1ch, 1dc in each dc of previous row, then 1dc in each ch to end; cut yarn and fasten off.

🖤 🖤 🖤 For larger sizes – and for any baby who has started to walk – it is advisable to add non-slip soles. For instructions, see page 154. 🖤 🖤 🖤

STRAP OF RIGHT SHOE

Starting at centre back, count 5[6:7:8] sts to the right of this point along top edge of shoe and join yarn to this stitch.

Foundation row: Work 1dc into marked st and 1dc into each of next 9[11:13:15] sts along top edge; turn.

Row 1: Make 25[28:31:32]ch, work 1dc in 2nd ch from hook, 1dc in each ch, then 1dc in each dc of previous row; cut yarn and fasten off.

♥ ♥ ♥ **For an interesting effect, when joining the sole and upper parts of the shoe, you could work the round of slip stitches in a contrasting colour.** ♥ ♥ ♥

FINISHING

Weave in yarn ends on straps, then attach snap fasteners at ends of straps, to fasten, following the manufacturer's instructions (see page 145).

♥ ♥ ♥ These gorgeous booties have so much potential to be made in many different colourways. Being so quick to make, why not make them in a whole array of colours? ♥ ♥ ♥

Gingham check

Made from crisp cotton and open at the front, these summer specials give little toes plenty of wriggle room during outings in the fresh air.

Size

To fit sizes 0–3[3–6:6–9:9–12] months
See size guide on pages 154–5

Pattern note

Seam allowances are $1/4$in (6mm) unless otherwise stated.

Pattern pieces

You will need the following pattern pieces from the pull-out sheet.

8 Front · cut 2 in gingham and 2 in lining fabric

9 Back · cut 2 in gingham and 2 in lining fabric

10 Sole · cut 2 in gingham and 2 in lining fabric

Materials and equipment

- Piece of 100% cotton dress-weight fabric, approximately $15^3/_4$ x 12in (40 x 30cm), in black and white gingham
- Piece of 100% cotton dress-weight fabric, approximately $15^3/_4$ x 12in (40 x 30cm), in red and white spot print, for lining
- Sewing needle
- Sewing thread, in white
- $2^1/_2$yd (2.25m) of 1in (25mm) bias binding, in black and white gingham
- Sewing machine (optional)

1 Trace the pattern pieces listed on page 34 from the pull-out sheet on to tracing paper and cut out to make templates (see page 134). Use the templates to cut two fronts, two backs and two soles each from the gingham and the spot print. Pair these with wrong sides together and baste them, stitching within the seam allowance.

2 Use bias binding to bind the two long edges of the front straps and the two short edges of the backs.

3 Pin the fronts to the soles, with the seam allowance on the outside and lining up the front edge to the marked point on the sole. Baste, then stitch in place by hand or machine.

4 Position each back piece, once again having the seam allowance on the outside and lining up the centre of each back to the centre back of each sole, and overlapping the front corners over the front pieces. Pin, baste and stitch.

5 Use bias binding to bind the seam allowance all round the base, starting and ending at the point where back and front pieces overlap at the side.

6 Cut the remaining bias binding in half and use one piece to bind the top back edge of each shoe, lining up the centre of each piece of binding to the centre back on each shoe, with the free ends of the bias binding forming ties. Tie these in a neat bow, trimming off any extra length.

♥ ♥ ♥ Look out for ready-made cotton bias binding in a variety of fabrics – not just plain colours but checks and prints. If you find it difficult to source interesting binding, you can make your own by cutting bias strips from fabric. Fold a square or rectangle diagonally to create a guideline, then use a long ruler to measure strips twice the width you want your finished binding to be. You will need to fold the strips: the best way to do this is to buy a small gadget called a tape maker, which makes this process very easy. ♥ ♥ ♥

Gingham check

Elfin boots

These cheeky and cheerful pointed-toe booties are just the thing for your little imp to create some mischief in.

Size

To fit sizes 0–6[6–12:12–18] months
See size guide on pages 154–5

Tension

26 sts and 34 rows to 4in (10cm),
measured over stocking stitch,
using 3.25mm needles. Use larger or
smaller needles if necessary to obtain
correct tension.

Materials and equipment

• 1 x 50g ball MillaMia Naturally Soft
  Merino yarn in shade 142 Daisy Yellow (A)
• 1 x 50g ball MillaMia Naturally Soft
  Merino yarn in shade 141 Grass (B)
• 1 pair of 3.25mm (UK10:US3) knitting
  needles
• 2 x 3mm (UK11:US2/3) double-pointed
  knitting needles
• 2 stitch holders and a safety pin
• Tapestry needle

Bootie (make 2)

CUFF EDGING

Using 3.25mm knitting needles and yarn A, cast on 4 sts.

Row 1 (WS): Knit.
Row 2: K2, yfwd, k2 (5 sts).
Row 3: Knit.
Row 4: K3, yfwd, k2 (6 sts).
Row 5: Knit.
Row 6: K4, yfwd, k2 (7 sts).
Row 7: Knit.
Row 8: K5, yfwd, k2 (8 sts).
Row 9: Knit.
Row 10: Knit.
Row 11: Cast off 4 sts, knit to end.
Rep rows 2–11 a further 6[7:8] times.
Cast off.

LEG AND UPPER

Using 3.25mm knitting needles and yarn B, pick up and knit 35[41:47] sts along straight edge of cuff edging.

Row 1: Knit.
Row 2: K1, *yfwd, k2tog; rep from * to end.
Beg with a knit row, work 20[24:28] rows in st st.

❤ ❤ ❤ **This soft wool yarn is not a standard weight but falls somewhere between 4-ply and DK. If you decide to substitute another yarn, it is essential that you check the tension.** ❤ ❤ ❤

Next row: K2, (k2tog, k4[5:6]) 5 times, k2tog, k1[2:3] (29[35:41] sts).
Next row: Purl.
Next row (eyelets): K1, *yfwd, k2tog; rep from * to end.
Next row: Purl.

INSTEP

Row 1: Knit 20[23:26]; turn and leave rem sts on a holder.
Row 2: P11, turn and mark base of last st worked; leave rem sts on a holder.
Beg with a knit row, work 4[6:8] rows on these 11 sts.
Next row: K2tog, k to last 2 sts, k2tog.

Next row: Purl.

Next row: Knit.

Next row: Purl.

Rep last 4 rows until 3 sts rem.

Next row: Sl1, k2tog, psso; leave rem st on a safety pin.

With RS facing, rejoin yarn to marked st, pick up and knit 16[18:20] sts evenly up edge, knit 1 st from safety pin, pick up and knit 16[18:20] sts down opposite edge, then knit 9[12:15] sts from holder (42[49:56] sts).

Next row: P42[49:56], then purl 9[12:15] sts from holder (51[61:71] sts).

Beg with a knit row, work 6[8:10] rows in st st.

SHAPE SOLE

Row 1: K2, sl1, k1, psso, k18[23:28], k2tog, k3, sl1, k1, psso, k18[23:28], k2tog, k2 (47[57:67] sts).

Row 2: Purl.

Row 3: K2, sl1, k1, psso, k16[21:26], k2tog, k3, sl1, k1, psso, k16[21:26], k2tog, k2 (43[53:63] sts).

Row 4: Purl.

Row 5: K2, sl1, k1, psso, k14[19:24], k2tog, k3, sl1, k1, psso, k14[19:24], k2tog, k2 (39[49:59] sts).

Row 6: Purl.

Row 7: K2, sl1, k1, psso, k12[17:22], k2tog, k3, sl1, k1, psso, k12[17:22], k2tog, k2 (35[45:55] sts).

Cast off purlwise.

I-cord (make 2)

Using 3mm double-pointed knitting needles and yarn B, cast on 2 sts.

Row 1: K2; do not turn but slide sts to other end of needle.

Rep this row 95[100:105] times more; cast off.

Making up

Fold boot in half, with right sides together, and oversew or graft seam along centre of sole. Stitch back seam, then sew short edges of cuff together. Weave in all remaining yarn ends. Turn right sides out and fold top hem over along eyelet row.

Beginning at centre front, thread cord through eyelet holes around base of leg and tie in a bow to fasten.

Little duckling

For outings in the pram on a chilly day, bright sunny yellow booties will provide both entertainment and warmth.

Size

To fit sizes 0–6[6–12:12–18] months
See size guide on pages 154–5

Tension

24 sts and 36 rows to 4in (10cm), measured over stocking stitch, using 3.25mm needles. Use larger or smaller needles if necessary to obtain correct tension.

Materials and equipment

• 1 x 50g ball MillaMia Naturally Soft Merino yarn in shade 142 Daisy Yellow (A)
• Small amount of DK yarn in orange (B)
• Small amount of DK or tapestry yarn in black
• 1 pair of 3.25mm (UK10:US3) needles
• 1 pair of size 3mm (UK11:US2/3) knitting needles
• Tapestry needle
• Small amount of polyester toy stuffing

♥ ♥ ♥ This soft wool yarn is not a standard weight but falls somewhere between a 4-ply and DK. If you decide to substitute another yarn, it is essential that you check the tension. ♥ ♥ ♥

Main piece (make 2)

Using 3.25mm needles and yarn A, cast on 35[45:55] sts.

Row 1: Knit.

Row 2: K1, (m1, k16[21:26], m1, k1) twice (39[49:59] sts).

Row 3: Knit.

Row 4: K1, (m1, k18[23:28], m1, k1) twice (43[53:63] sts).

Row 5: Knit.

Row 6: K1, (m1, k20[25:30], m1, k1) twice (47[57:67] sts).

Row 7: Knit.

Row 8: K1, (m1, k22[27:32], m1, k1) twice (51[61:71] sts).

Row 9: Knit.

Row 10: K1, (m1, k24[29:34], m1, k1) twice (55[65:75] sts).

Row 11: Knit.

Row 12: Knit.

Row 13: Purl.

Rep rows 12 and 13 a further 2[3:4] times.

INSTEP

Row 1: K30[35:40], sl1, k1, psso, k1, turn.

Row 2: P7, p2tog, p1, turn.

Row 3: K8, sl1, k1, psso, k1, turn.

Row 4: P9, p2tog, p1, turn

Row 5: K10, sl1, k1, psso, k1, turn.

Row 6: P11, p2tog, turn.

Row 7: K11, sl1, k1, psso, turn.

Rep rows 6 and 7 a further 6[7:8] times, then row 6 once more (35[43:51] sts).

Next row: Knit to end.

Next row: Purl.

Next row (eyelets): K1, *yfwd, k2tog; rep from * to end.

Beg with a purl row, work 15[17:19] rows in st st.

Next row: K1, *yfwd, k2tog; rep from * to end.

Beg with a purl row, work 5 rows in st st. Cast off.

Head (make 2)

Using 3.25mm needles and yarn A, cast on 12 sts.

Row 1: Purl.

Row 2: K1, (m1, k2) 5 times, m1, k1 (18 sts).

Row 3: Purl.

Row 4: K2, (m1, k3) 5 times, m1, k1 (24 sts).

Row 5: Purl.

Row 6: K2, (m1, k4) 5 times, m1, k2 (30 sts).

Beg with a purl row, work 5 rows in st st.

Row 12: (K3, k2tog) 6 times (24 sts).

Row 13: Purl.

Row 14: (K2, k2tog) 6 times (18 sts).

Row 15: Purl.
Row 16: (K1, k2tog) 6 times (12 sts).
Row 17: (P2tog) 6 times.
Cut yarn and thread tail through rem 6 sts.

Beak (make 2)

Using 3mm needles and yarn B, cast on 8 sts.
Beg with a purl row, work 7 rows in st st.
Row 8: K1, sl1, k1, psso, k2, k2tog, k1 (6 sts).
Row 9: Purl.
Row 10: K1, sl1, k1, psso, k2tog, k1 (4 sts).
Row 11: P1, p2tog, p1 (3 sts).
Row 12: K1, inc1, k1 (4 sts).
Row 13: Purl.
Row 14: K1, (inc1) twice, k1 (6 sts).
Row 15: Purl.
Row 16: K1, inc1, k2, inc1, k1 (8 sts).
Beg with a purl row, work 7 rows in st st.
Cast off.

Cord (make 2)

Using 3mm needles and yarn A, cast on 50 sts using simple cast-on method, then slip sts off needle and fasten off last st.

Making up

Fold boot in half, with right sides together, and stitch back seam, then oversew seam along centre of sole. Fold top hem to inside along eyelet row, which forms a picot edge, and slipstitch cast-off edge in place. Turn right sides out.

Pull up yarn on last row of head and fasten off, then stitch seam, leaving lower edge open. Stuff head quite firmly (but without stretching knitted fabric too much), then stitch one head to front of each boot. Fold beak in half with right sides together and stitch side seams in backstitch. Turn right sides out and stitch cast-on and cast-off edges to front of head. Make a small bundle of yellow yarn by winding it around your fingers and tying firmly around the centre, then stitch the centre of the bundle firmly to the top of the head, cut through all the loops and trim the ends. Thread tapestry needle with a length of black yarn and embroider eyes in satin stitch (see page 135).

Beginning at centre back, thread cord through eyelet holes around base of leg and tie in a bow.

Cosy slippers

Made in warm and cosy felt, with non-slip soles for extra grip, these are just right for slipping tired little feet into for a soothing bedtime story.

Size

To fit sizes 12–15[15–18:18–24:24–36] months. See size guide on pages 154–5

Pattern note

Seam allowances are $1/4$in (6mm) unless otherwise stated.

Pattern pieces

You will need the following pattern pieces from the pull-out sheet.

11 Upper · cut 2 in felt

12 Sole · cut 2 in felt and 2 in non-slip fabric

Materials and equipment

- Piece of wool or wool-viscose felt, approximately $15^3/_4$ x 12in (40 x 30cm), in grey
- Piece of non-slip fabric, approximately 7 x 7in (18 x 18cm)
- Sewing needle
- Crewel needle
- 6-stranded embroidery thread, in white, pale green and yellow
- Sewing thread, in colour to match felt
- Sewing machine (optional)

10

1 Trace the pattern pieces listed on page 46 from the pull-out sheet on to tracing paper and cut out to make templates (see page 134). Use the templates to cut two soles and two uppers from felt and two soles from felt and non-slip fabric. Transfer the embroidery motif on to each slipper front. To do this, either trace the motif on to paper using a transfer pen or pencil, then transfer to the fabric using a hot iron, or copy the shapes freehand with a pen or pencil. Using three strands of embroidery thread, embroider the flower petals in white using detached chain stitch (lazy daisy); the stems in pale green using chain stitch, and the flower centres in yellow French knots (see page 137).

2 Place the two short straight edges of the upper together and stitch to form back seam (seam is on inside of shoe). Press the seam open, then, to keep seam allowance on back seam flat, topstitch on either side of seam.

3 Pin each felt sole to a non-slip sole and stitch all round, through both thicknesses, within the seam allowance.

4 Pin the upper to the sole with the seam allowance on the outside of each shoe. Baste, then stitch the sole firmly to the upper by hand or machine.

5 Using three strands of white embroidery thread, work blanket stitch (see page 136) all round edge of each shoe, inserting the needle through both thicknesses of fabric.

6 Still using three strands of white embroidery thread, work blanket stitch all round top edge of shoe, for a neat finish.

7 Fold top edge of shoe over to the outside and secure in place with a couple of stitches on the back seam.

♥ ♥ ♥ **Felt is easy to use and, as it does not fray, does not require hemming. Make sure you choose a pure wool or wool-viscose felt – do not use craft felt. You can make your own felt by washing a pure wool jumper in the washing machine at 104°F (40°C), which will cause the knitted fabric to shrink and harden. Leave the resulting fabric to dry on a flat surface and press with a steam iron to smooth out any wrinkles before cutting out and stitching.** ♥ ♥ ♥

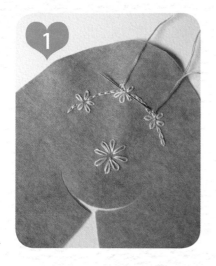

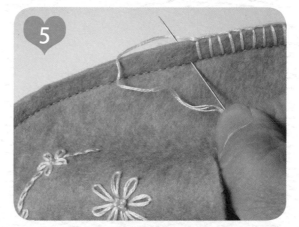

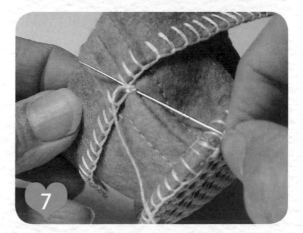

Princess jewels

Perfect for those fun-filled dressing-up days, these golden slippers with silk linings will be popular with every little princess.

Size

To fit sizes 6–9[9–12:12–15:15–18] months
See size guide on pages 154–5

Pattern note

Seam allowances are $1/4$in (6mm) unless otherwise stated.

Pattern pieces

You will need the following pattern pieces from the pull-out sheet.

13 Upper · cut 2 in leatherette and 2 in silk lining

14 Left sole · cut 1 in leatherette and 1 in silk lining

15 Right sole · cut 1 in leatherette and 1 in silk lining

Materials and equipment

- Piece of leatherette, approximately $15^3/_4$ x 12in (40 x 30cm), in gold
- Piece of habutai silk lining fabric, approximately $15^3/_4$ x 12in (40 x 30cm), in yellow
- Sewing needle
- Sewing thread, yellow
- 2 snap fasteners
- 2 decorative buttons (optional)
- Sewing machine (optional)

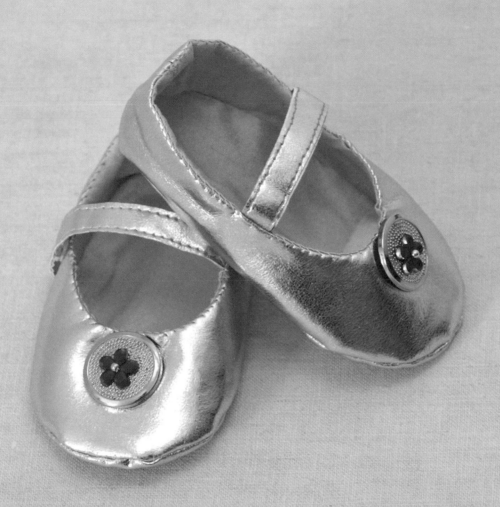

11

1 Trace the pattern pieces listed on page 50 from the pull-out sheet on to tracing paper and cut out to make templates (see page 134). Use the templates to cut two soles and two uppers from both the leatherette and the silk lining and four straps, each measuring 3½ by ³⁄₈in (9 x 1cm), from the leatherette only. Place the two short straight edges of the upper together and stitch to form back seam (seam is on inside of shoe). Use your fingers to press the back seam of the shoe open, then, with right sides together, baste then stitch the sole to the upper with the seam allowance on the inside of each shoe.

2 Snip into the seam allowance at the front of each shoe, around the curves, then turn right sides out.

3 For each shoe, place two strap pieces together, right sides out, and topstitch close to edges. Stitch the end of the strap to the inner edge of the shoe.

4 Stitch the back seam of the lining, then pin, baste and stitch the upper part of lining to the sole piece of the lining and snip curves. Place the lining inside the shoe, then turn under ³⁄₁₆in (5mm) on the top edge of both lining and shoe, and baste.

5 Slipstitch top edges of main fabric and lining together using small, neat stitches. (You may find it easier to turn each shoe inside out to do this.) Finally, stitch snap fasteners in place on the end of each strap and the side of each shoe, and stitch a decorative button securely to the front of each shoe, if you wish.

♥ ♥ ♥ **Leatherette has the appearance of leather, but it is easier to stitch and does not require special needles or threads. It is available in a choice of colours, including metallics such as the gold used here.** ♥ ♥ ♥

Lacy sandals

Light, crisp cotton is the perfect choice for a baby's summer shoes. These ones are suitable for everyday wear but special enough for a christening or other dress-up event.

Size

To fit sizes 0–3[3–6:6–9] months
See size guide on pages 154–5

Tension

22 sts and 34 rows to 4in (10cm), measured over rows of double crochet, using 3.50mm hook. Use a larger or smaller hook if necessary to obtain correct tension.

Materials and equipment

• 1 x 50g ball Rowan Siena 4-ply yarn in shade 0651 White
• 3.50mm (UK9:USE-4) crochet hook
• Stitch marker
• Tapestry needle
• 48in (1.2m) narrow white ribbon or cotton tape
• Sewing needle and white thread

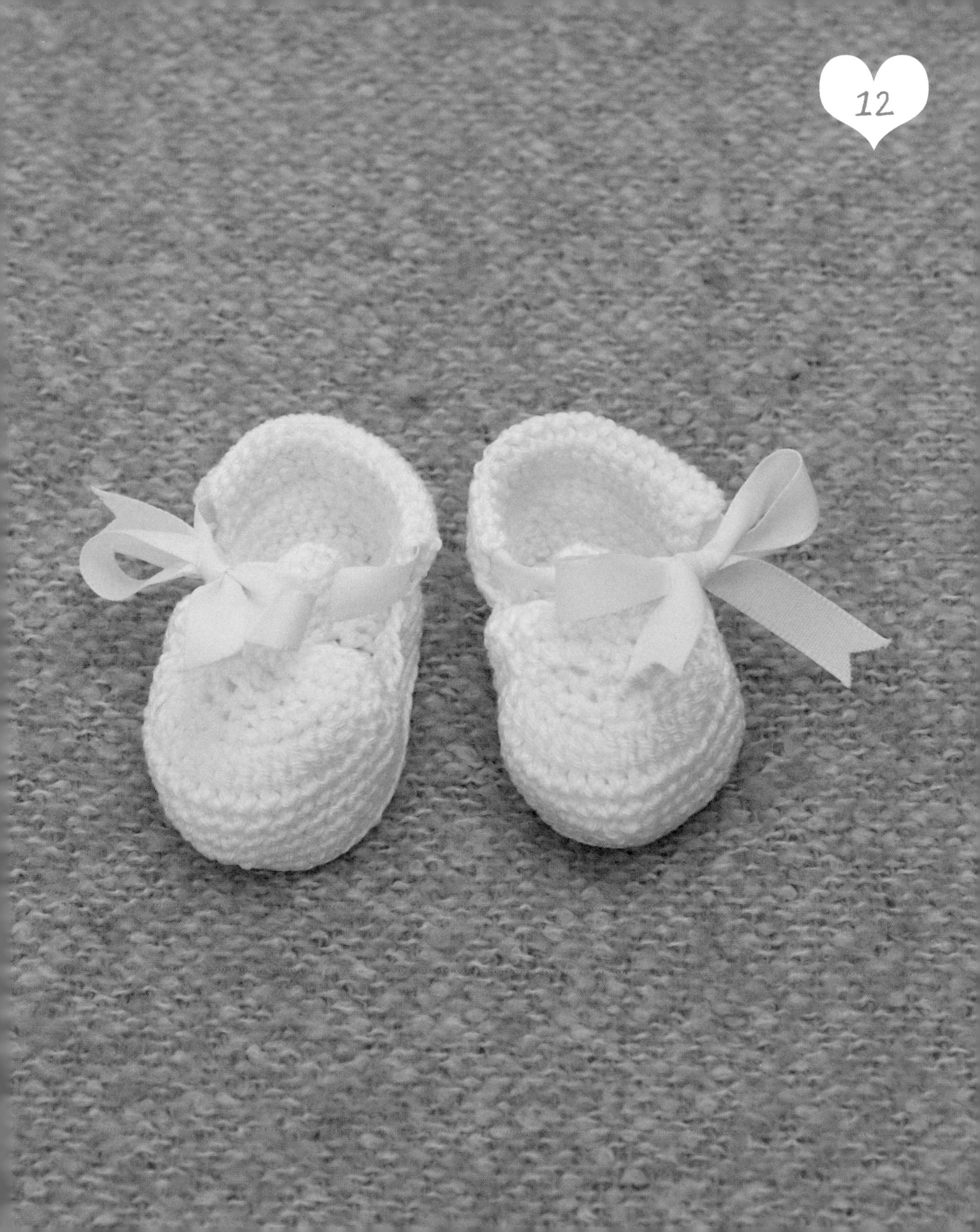
12

Upper (make 2)

Foundation row: Make 2ch; work 3dc in 2nd ch from hook; turn (3 sts).

Row 1: 1ch (does not count as st), 2dc in each dc of previous row; turn (6 sts).

Row 2: 1ch, 2dc in each dc of previous row; turn (12 sts).

Row 3: 3ch (counts as 1tr), 1tr in same place, (1tr in next dc, 2tr in next dc) 5 times, 1tr in last dc; do not turn but work 11dc along straight edge, working last 3dc in 3ch at start of row; turn (21 sts).

Row 4: 1ch, 1dc in each of 11dc on straight edge; turn.

Row 5: 1ch, 1dc in each of first 5dc on straight edge, miss 1dc, 1dc in each of next 5dc; do not turn.

SIDES

Round 1: Work 2 more dc in last st worked and place marker in first of these, then 1dc in 3rd of 3ch and in each of 17tr around curved edge of toe, 2dc in same place as 1st dc of row 5, 26[30:34]ch; join with sl st to marked st (48[52:56] sts).

Round 2: 1ch, 1dc in each dc of previous round.

Rep round 2 a further 1[2:3] time(s).

Next round: 1ch, 1dc in each of next 9dc, (dc2tog) twice, 1dc in each of next 20[22:24]dc, (dc2tog) twice, 1dc in each of next 11[13:15]dc; join with sl st to 1st dc of round (44[48:52] sts).

Next round: 1ch, 1dc in each of next 8dc, (dc2tog) twice, 1dc in each of next 32[36:40]dc; join with sl st to 1st dc of round (42[46:50] sts).

Cut yarn and fasten off.

Sole (make 2)

Foundation chain: Make 11[13:15]ch.

Round 1: 1dc in 2nd ch from hook, 2dc in next ch, 1dc in next ch, 1htr in each of next 3[4:5]ch, 1tr in each of next 3[4:5]ch, 7tr in last ch; do not turn but work back along opposite side of foundation chain as follows: 1tr in each of next 3[4:5]ch,

1htr in each of next 3[4:5]ch, 1dc in next ch, 2dc in next ch, 1dc in next ch, join with sl st in 1st dc of round (27[31:35] sts).
Round 2: 3ch (counts as 1tr), 2tr in each of next 3 sts, 1tr in each of next 6[8:10] sts, 2tr in each of next 3 sts, 3tr in next st, 2tr in each of next 3 sts, 1tr in each of next 6[8:10] sts, 2tr in each of next 3 sts, 1tr in next dc, join with sl st to 3rd of 3ch at beg of round (42[46:50] sts).
Fasten off but do not cut yarn. Line up centre back of upper with centre back of sole and work 1sl st in each pair of sts to join, inserting hook in back loop only of each st.

Back casing

Foundation row: With RS facing, counting from straight edge of toe cap, miss 5[6:7] ch on upper edge, join yarn to next st and work 1ch, 1dc in same st and 1dc in each of next 15[17:19]ch; turn (16[18:20] sts).
Row 1: 1ch, 1dc in each dc of previous row.
Rep row 1 a further 4 times.
Cut yarn and fasten off.

Tab

Foundation chain: Make 9ch.
Foundation row: 1dc in 2nd ch from hook, 1dc in each of next 8ch (8 sts).
Row 1: 1ch, 1dc in each dc of previous row.
Cut yarn and fasten off.

Making up

Fold back casing to RS and oversew sts on last row to base of casing. Cut ribbon or tape in half and thread one piece through casing on each shoe. Weave in all remaining yarn ends.

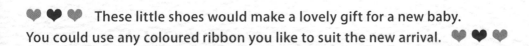

♥ ♥ ♥   These little shoes would make a lovely gift for a new baby. You could use any coloured ribbon you like to suit the new arrival.   ♥ ♥ ♥

Ballet slippers

These little pumps are very simple to knit in luxurious alpaca yarn. Add soft velvet ribbon ties in a shade to match the yarn.

Size

To fit sizes 0–6[6–9:9–12:12–18] months
See size guide on pages 154–5

Tension

22 sts and 40 rows to 4in (10cm), measured over garter stitch, using 3.25mm needles. Use larger or smaller needles if necessary to obtain correct tension.

Materials and equipment

• 1 x 50g ball Artesano DK 100% Alpaca yarn in shade CA13 Sweet Pea (A)
• 1 pair of 3.25mm (UK10:US3) needles
• Stitch holder
• Tapestry needle
• 1$\frac{1}{4}$yd (1m) of $\frac{3}{8}$in (10mm)-wide double-faced velvet ribbon
• Sewing needle
• Sewing thread to match ribbon

13

♥ ♥ ♥ Luxurious double-faced velvet ribbon has been used on the shoes shown here – but you could use single-faced velvet, satin or sheer organza ribbon instead, if you prefer. ♥ ♥ ♥

Shoe (make 2)

Cast on 37[41:45:49] sts.

Row 1: Knit each st tbl.

Row 2: Knit.

Row 3: K1, m1, k17[19:21:23], m1, k1, m1, k17[19:21:23], m1, k1 (41[45:49:53] sts).

Row 4: Knit.

Row 5: K1, m1, k19[21:23:25], m1, k1, m1, k19[21:23:25], m1, k1 (45[49:53:57] sts).

Row 6: Knit.

Row 7: K22[24:26:28], m1, k1, m1, k22[24:26:28] (47[51:55:59] sts).

Knit 5[7:9:11] rows.

Next row: K21[23:25:27], sl1, k1, psso, k1, k2tog, k21[23:25:27] (45[49:53:57] sts).

Next row: Knit.

Next row: K20[22:24:26], sl1, k1, psso, k1, k2tog, k20[22:24:26] (43[47:51:55] sts).

Next row: Knit.

Next row: K19[21:23:25], sl1, k1, psso, k1, k2tog, k19[21:23:25] (41[45:49:53] sts).

SHAPE FIRST SIDE OF HEEL

Next row: K9[11:13:15] and place on holder, cast off 23 sts, knit to end.

Knit 3 rows on these 9[11:13:15] sts.

Cast off.

SHAPE SECOND SIDE OF HEEL

Rejoin yarn to inner edge of sts on holder and knit 4 rows.

Cast off.

Making up

Fold shoe in half, with right sides together, and stitch back seam, then oversew seam along centre of sole. Weave in all yarn ends neatly. Turn right sides out.

Cut four lengths of ribbon each measuring 8³/₄[9:9¹/₂:9³/₄]in (22[23:24:25]cm). On each piece, fold under approximately ³/₁₆in (5mm) at one end and, using matching sewing thread, securely stitch one on each side of each shoe.

Puppy dog

Soft and supple, with cute dog faces, these shoes have puppy appeal and are suitable for both boys and girls.

Size

To fit sizes 12–15[15–18:18–24:24–36] months. See size guide on pages 154–5

Pattern note

Seam allowances are ¼in (6mm) unless otherwise stated.

Pattern pieces

You will need the following pattern pieces from the pull-out sheet.

16 **Toe** · cut 2 in cream suedette
17 **Back** · cut 2 in grey-brown suedette
18 **Face** · cut 2 in grey-brown suedette
19 **Sole** · cut 2 in cream suedette and 2 in non-slip fabric

Materials and equipment

- Piece of suedette, approximately 15¾ x 12in (40 x 30cm), in grey-brown
- Piece of suedette, approximately 15¾ x 12in (40 x 30cm), in cream
- Small scrap of leatherette, in black, for nose
- Piece of non-slip fabric, approximately 7 x 7in (18 x 18cm), in white, for base of sole
- 1yd (90cm) white cotton tape
- Sewing needle
- Sewing thread to match fabric
- Embroidery thread, in black
- Four small black buttons, for eyes
- Sewing machine (optional)

14

1 Using the templates listed on page 62 from the pull-out sheet, cut out two faces and two backs from grey-brown suedette, two soles and two toe caps from cream fabric, and two sole bases from suedette and non-slip fabric. On the toe caps, turn under $1/4$in (6mm) on each straight edge to form a narrow hem, and stitch.

2 Position one face piece on each of the toe caps and stitch in place, by hand or machine. Cut two nose shapes from black leatherette and stitch in place in the centre of each face.

3 From spare grey-brown suedette, cut two bias strips, each 1in (25mm) wide and long enough to bind the shorter edge of the back (heel) piece. Fold in half, position over edge of back piece, and baste; then trim ends. Place suedette sole and non-slip sole pieces together, right sides out, and baste all round within seam allowance.

4 Pin the back piece to the sole on each shoe, with the seam allowance on the inside, and lining up the front edge of each back piece to the marked point on the sole. Baste, then stitch in place by hand or machine.

5 Position each toe cap, once again having the seam allowance on the inside and lining up the centre front of each toe cap to the centre front of each sole, and overlapping the ends of the hemmed edge over the ends of the back piece. Pin, baste and stitch.

6 Turn right sides out and stitch buttons in place on toe caps, for eyes. Cut the cotton tape into two equal lengths and thread through casing on back of shoe; tie ends in a neat bow.

♥ ♥ ♥ **Suedette has been used to make the shoes pictured here. It is easy to cut and stitch, and bias-cut edges tend not to fray. You may prefer to use a soft leather or suede instead: offcuts are inexpensive to buy. For stitching real leather (as opposed to suedette or leatherette) by hand or machine, use a special leather needle; this has a really sharp point that cuts easily through the material. ♥ ♥ ♥**

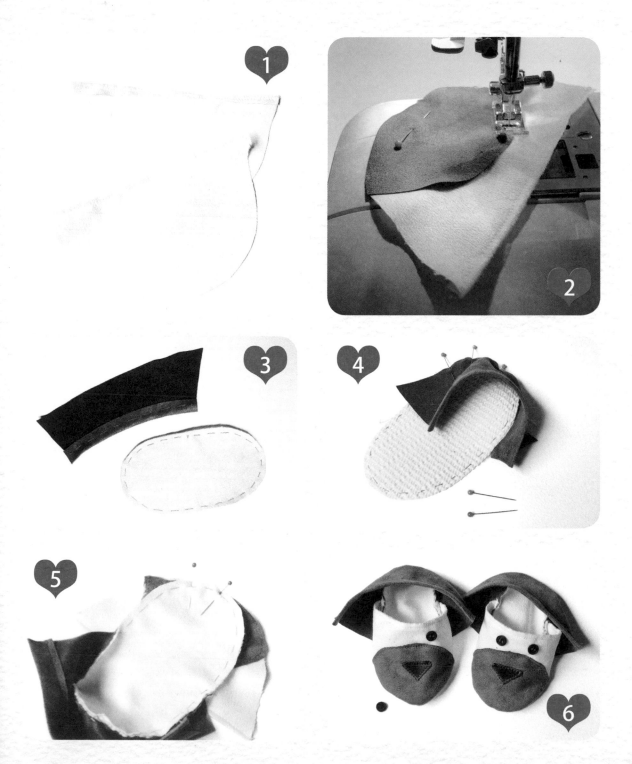

Strappy sandals

Cute and cool, these slippers masquerade as sandals, with open fronts to allow sun-kissed feet to stretch and curl.

Size
To fit sizes 12–15[15–18:18–24:24–36] months. See size guide on pages 154–5

Tension
18 sts and 10 rows to 4in (10cm), measured over rows of double crochet, using 4.00mm hook. Use a larger or smaller hook if necessary to obtain correct tension.

Pattern pieces
You will need the following pattern pieces from the pull-out sheet.
20 **Sole** · cut 2 in soft leather

Materials and equipment
- 1 x 50g ball Rowan Belle Organic by Amy Butler DK yarn in shade 023 Bluebell (A)
- 1 x 50g ball Rowan Belle Organic by Amy Butler DK yarn in shade 013 Moonflower (B)
- 4.00mm (UK8:USG-6) crochet hook
- Piece of soft leather approximately 7 x 7in (18 x 18cm)
- Leather punch
- Tapestry needle
- 4 small buttons, orange
- 4 snap fasteners
- Sewing needle and thread

15

Sole and upper (make 2)

Using templates listed on page 66 from the pull-out sheet, cut two soles from soft leather and punch 27[31:35:39] holes, as indicated on the pattern pieces.

Foundation round: Using 4.00mm crochet hook and A, join yarn to hole at centre back of sole and work 1ch (does not count as st), 1dc in same place, then 2dc in each hole to end; join with sl st to 1st dc (53[61:69:77] sts).

Round 1: 1ch (does not count as st), 1dc in each dc of previous round; join with sl st in 1st dc.

Rep round 1 2[3:4:5] times more.

Next round: 1 ch, 1dc in 1st dc, 1dc in next dc, dc2tog over next 2dc, 1dc in each of next 14[18:22:26]dc, (dc2tog, 1dc) twice, (2dctog) twice, (1dc, 2dctog) twice, 1dc in each of next 14[18:22:26]dc, dc2tog over next 2 sts, 1dc, sl st to 1st dc (45[53:61:69] sts).

Cut yarn and fasten off.

Rear strap of left sandal

With RS facing, starting at centre back and counting dc at centre back as 1st st, count 12 sts to right and rejoin yarn A to this st.

Row 1: Using yarn A, work 1ch (does not count as st), 1dc in same st, 1dc in each of next 2[2:3:3] sts; turn (3[3:4:4] sts).

Row 2: 1ch, 1dc in each dc of previous row.

Rep row 2 a further 10[11:12:13] times more.

Next row: 1ch, miss 1dc, 2[2:3:3]dctog over next 2[2:3:3]dc; cut yarn and fasten off.

Front strap of left sandal

With RS facing, starting at 12th st, count 6 sts to right, rejoin yarn A to this st and work strap in same way as centre strap but rep row 2 a further 9[10:11:12] times instead.

Rear strap of right sandal

With RS facing, starting at centre back and counting dc at centre back as 1st st, count 10 sts to left and rejoin yarn A to this st, then work centre strap as given for left sandal.

Front strap of right sandal

Leave 3dc unworked to left of centre strap, rejoin yarn to next st along and work front strap as given for left sandal.

Flower (make 4)

Using yarn B, make 4ch and join with a sl st to 1st ch to make a ring.

Round 1: 1ch (does not count as st), 6dc in ring; join with sl st to 1st dc of round (6 sts).

Round 2: (3ch, sl st into next dc) 6 times; cut yarn, leaving a tail, and fasten off.

Making up

Stitch one flower to the end of each strap and stitch a button in the centre of each. Stitch one half of a snap fastener to the end of each strap on the underside, and the corresponding part of each snap fastener to the opposite side of each strap. Weave in all yarn ends neatly.

Crossover pumps

These little shoes are easy and quick to knit in soft DK yarn; the crossover straps, buttoned on both sides, help to keep them firmly on your baby's feet.

Size

To fit sizes 9–12[12–18:18–24:24–36] months
See size guide on pages 154–5

Tension

22 sts and 40 rows to 4in (10cm), measured over garter stitch, using 3.25mm needles. Use larger or smaller needles if necessary to obtain correct tension.

Materials and equipment

- 1 x 50g ball Sublime Baby Cashmerino Silk DK yarn in shade 162 Pinkaboo
- 1 pair of 3.25mm (UK10:US3) needles
- Stitch holder
- Tapestry needle
- 4 small (approx $1/2$–$5/8$in/12–15mm) buttons
- Sewing needle and thread

16

Shoe (make 2)

Cast on 39[43:47:51] sts.
Row 1: Knit.
Row 2: K1, inc1, k16[18:20:22], inc1, k1, inc1, k16[18:20:22], inc1, k1 (43[47:51:55] sts).
Row 3: Knit.
Row 4: K2, inc1, k16[18:20:22], inc1, k3, inc1, k16[18:20:22], inc1, k2 (47[51:55:59] sts).
Row 5: Knit.
Row 6: K3, inc1, k16[18:20:22], inc1, k5, inc1, k16[18:20:22], inc1, k3 (51[55:59:63] sts).
Row 7: Knit.
Row 8: K4, inc1, k16[18:20:22], inc1, k7, inc1, k16[18:20:22], inc1, k4 (55[59:63:67] sts).
Knit 13[13:15:15] rows.
Next row: K19[21:23:25], (sl1, k1, psso) 4 times, k1, (k2tog) 4 times, k19[21:23:25] (47[51:55:59] sts).
Next row: Knit.
Next row: K11[12:13:14] sts and place on stitch holder, cast off 25[27:29:31] sts,

♥ ♥ ♥ Make a few pairs of shoes in the smallest size, in an assortment of colours, and pack them in a box with tissue paper as a gift for a new baby. ♥ ♥ ♥

then knit rem 10[11:12:13] sts. There are 11[12:13:14] sts on needle.

MAKE FIRST STRAP
Row 1: Knit.
Row 2: Cast on 13[14:15:16] sts, k to end (24[26:28:30] sts).
Row 3 (buttonhole): K21[23:25:27], yfwd, k2tog, k1.
Row 4: Knit.
Cast off.

MAKE SECOND STRAP
Row 1: Cast on 13[14:15:16] sts, transfer needle with sts to right hand, then knit stitches from holder (24[26:28:30] sts).
Row 2: Knit.
Row 3 (buttonhole): K1, k2tog, yfwd, k21[23:25:27].
Row 4: Knit.
Cast off.

♥ ♥ ♥ This cashmere and silk blend yarn is very soft and a good choice for a baby's delicate skin. One ball of yarn is enough to make two pairs of shoes in the smallest size. ♥ ♥ ♥

Baby Booties and Slippers

Making up

Fold shoe in half, with right sides together, and stitch back seam, then oversew seam along centre of sole. Weave in all yarn ends neatly. Turn right sides out. Using matching sewing thread, securely stitch buttons of an appropriate size to the shoes, one on each side of each shoe.

♥ ♥ ♥ Add-on soles in fabric, leather or a non-slip material can easily be sewn on to any of the projects. See pages 152–3 for instructions. ♥ ♥ ♥

Seaside stripes

Woven striped cotton is light and crisp – ideal for outings in the pram on a summer's day when your baby needs to look smart and keep cool.

Size

To fit sizes 3–6[6–9:9–12:12–15] months
See size guide on pages 154–5

Pattern note

Seam allowances are $1/4$in (6mm) unless otherwise stated.

Pattern pieces

You will need the following pattern pieces from the pull-out sheet.

21 **Upper** · cut 4 in striped fabric
22 **Lining** · cut 2 in striped fabric
23 **Sole** · cut 4 in striped fabric

Materials and equipment

- Piece of 100% cotton dress-weight fabric, approximately $15^3/4$ x $19^3/4$in (40 x 50cm), in blue and white stripes
- Sewing needle
- Sewing thread, in white
- 2 snap fasteners, in clear plastic
- $19^3/4$in (50cm) of narrow ric-rac braid, in white
- Sewing machine (optional)

17

1 Cut four uppers (two for each shoe), two linings and four soles using the templates listed on page 74 from the pull-out sheet. Cut two straps, each measuring 3½ x 1in (9 x 2.5cm). Join the uppers in pairs along the front seam; press the seam flat.

2 Stitch the back seam on each upper for each shoe. Stitch the back seam on each lining.

3 Mark the centre front and centre back of two of the sole pieces and line these up with the front and back seams on the uppers. Pin, then baste together within the seam allowance. Pin and baste the remaining two sole pieces to the two linings.

4 Fold each strap in half lengthways and stitch, leaving one end open; then turn right sides out with the help of a long thin object such as a knitting needle.

5 On the top edge of the shoe, fold ³/₁₆in (5mm) to the inside and baste; do this on the two uppers and the two

linings. On each of the main parts of the shoe, stitch the open end of the strap to the inside centre of one side. (This will be on the left side for the right shoe and the right side for the left shoe.)

6 Pair up each upper with its lining, with wrong sides together, and slipstitch folded edges together using small, neat stitches.

7 Stitch the snap fasteners in place on the end of each strap and the side of the shoe. For a neat finishing touch, stitch ric-rac braid around the top edge of each shoe, starting and finishing just above the snap fastener.

♥ ♥ ♥   Cotton fabric in woven stripes is an excellent choice for cool summer pram shoes. But remember that cloth shoes do not offer any support, and fabric soles are slippery and so not suitable for babies who are walking. ♥ ♥ ♥

Baby Booties and Slippers

Watermelon slices

*Fruity and fun, these pull-on booties
have ties to secure them around the ankle
and styling that will make you smile.*

Size

To fit size 0–3[3–6:6–9] months
See size guide on pages 154–5

Tension

24 sts and 30 rows to 4in (10cm),
measured over rows of double crochet
using 3.00mm hook. Use a larger or
smaller hook if necessary to obtain
correct tension.

Materials and equipment

• 1 x 50g ball Rowan 4-ply cotton yarn
  in shade 133 Cheeky (A)
• 1 x 50g ball Rowan 4-ply cotton yarn
  in shade 135 Fennel (C)
• Small amount of Rowan 4-ply cotton
  yarn in shade 113 Bleached (B)
• 3.00mm (UK11:USC-2/D3) crochet hook
• Stitch marker
• Tapestry needle
• Black embroidery thread

18

Leg and instep (make 2)

Foundation chain: Using yarn A, make 27[31:35]ch.

Row 1: 1dc in 2nd ch from hook, 1dc in each ch to end (26[30:34] sts).

Row 2: 1ch (does not count as st), 1dc in each ch to end.

Rep row 2 a further 8[10:12] times.

Next row: 1ch, 1dc in 1st st, (1ch, miss 1 st, 1dc in next st) 12[14:16] times, 1dc in last st.

Next row: 1ch, 1dc in each dc and ch sp of previous row.

Next row: 1dc in 1st st, 1dc in each of next 16[18:20] sts; turn.

Next row: 1ch, 1dc in 1st st, 1dc in each of next 7 sts; turn (8dc).

Place marker in base of last st worked, then rep previous row 10[12:14] times.

Fasten off.

Remove marker and rejoin yarn to same place, then work 11[13:15] sts evenly along side of instep, inserting hook into row ends, then 1dc in each of 8 sts along top, 11[13:15]dc down opposite edge and 1dc in each of 9[11:13] sts on other side (48[56:64] sts).

Cut yarn and join in B.

Next row: 1ch, 1dc in each dc to end; turn. Rep previous row once more, then cut yarn and join in C.

Next row: 1ch, 1dc in each dc to end; turn. Rep previous row 2[3:4] times. Cut yarn and fasten off.

Sole (make 2)

Foundation chain: Using yarn C, make 8[9:10]ch.

Row 1: 1dc in 2nd ch from hook, 1dc in each ch to end; turn (7[8:9] sts).

Row 2: 1ch, 2dc in first dc, 1dc in each of next 5[6:7]dc, 2dc in last dc; turn (9[11:13] sts).

Row 3: 1ch, 2dc in first dc, 1dc in each of next 7[8:9]dc, 2dc in last dc; turn (11[13:15] sts).

Row 4: 1ch, 1dc in each dc to end; turn. Rep row 4 a further 16[20:24] times.

Next row: 1ch, dc2tog over first 2dc, 1dc in each of next 7[8:9]dc, dc2tog over last 2dc (9[11:13] sts).

Next row: 1ch, dc2tog over first 2dc, 1dc in each of next 5[6:7]dc, dc2tog over last 2dc (7[9:11] sts).

Cut yarn and fasten off.

Flat cord (make 2)

Make 2ch, then work 1dc in 1st of these 2ch; *turn work clockwise away from you so that second loop of dc just worked is uppermost, insert hook through both loops of this st and work 1dc, rep from * 80[84:88] times, or until cord is long enough to fit around leg and tie in a bow.

Making up

Stitch back seam, then stitch upper to sole. Thread tapestry needle with embroidery thread and embroider watermelon seeds on instep of each bootie. To embroider a seed, first embroider a detached chain stitch (see page 137), then work a single straight stitch inside the loop, to fill in the chain stitch. Repeat until you have a scattering of seeds. Starting at the centre front, thread one flat cord through the eyelet holes in each bootie and tie ends in a neat bow.

♥ ❤ ♥ **As an alternative to the crocheted cords, you could knit the cords; see page 145 for instructions.** ♥ ❤ ♥

Button boots

Perfect for cold-weather outings in the pushchair or cosy storytelling sessions on the sofa, these boots are crocheted in a ridged stitch, making them extra thick and warm.

Size

To fit sizes 6–9[9–12:12–15] months
See size guide on pages 154–5

Tension

20 sts and 28 rows to 4in (10cm), measured over rows of double crochet using a 3.50mm hook. Use a larger or smaller hook if necessary to obtain correct tension.

Materials and equipment

• 1 x 50g ball Artesano DK 100% Alpaca yarn in shade CA13 Sweet Pea
• 3.50mm (UK9:USE-4) crochet hook
• Tapestry needle
• 4 fabric-covered buttons

Pattern note

The attractive ridged pattern is achieved by inserting the crochet hook into the back loops of the stitches.

19

Right bootie

LEG AND INSTEP

Foundation chain: Make 35[39:43]ch.

Row 1: 1dc in 2nd ch from hook, 1dc in each ch to end (34[38:42] sts).

Row 2: 1ch (does not count as st), 1dc in each ch to end (remembering to insert the hook into the back loop only of each st).

Row 3: 1ch, 1dc in each dc to end.

Row 4: As row 3.

Row 5 (buttonhole): 1ch, 1dc in 1st st, 2ch, miss 2dc, 1dc in each dc to end.

Row 6: 1ch, 1dc in each st to end.

Rep row 6 a further 4[6:8] times.

Next row (buttonhole): 1ch, 1dc in 1st st, 2ch, miss 2dc, 1dc in each dc to end.

Rep row 6 a further 3 times.

Bring opposite edge around to form a cylinder, overlapping the edges, and line up the last 8 sts of the row just worked behind the first 8 sts and proceed as follows:

Work 1sl st, inserting hook through back loop of 1st st and the corresponding st behind; do the same with the next 7 pairs of sts (26[30:34] sts).

Next row: 1ch, 1dc in 1st st, 1dc in each of next 4 sts; turn.

Next row: 1ch, 1dc in 1st st, 1dc in each of next 7 sts; turn (8 sts).

Place marker in base of last st worked, then rep previous row 10[12:14] times. Cut yarn and fasten off.

Remove marker and rejoin yarn to same

place, then work 11[13:15] sts evenly along side of instep, inserting hook into row ends, then 1dc in each of 8 sts along top, 11[13:15]dc down opposite edge and 1dc in each of first 10[12:14] sts on other side.

Next row: 1ch, 1dc in each of next 23[27:31]dc, (dc2tog over next 2dc) twice, 1dc in each dc to end (48[56:64] sts).

Next row: 1ch, 1dc in each dc to end; turn.

Rep previous row a further 4[6:8] times. Cut yarn and fasten off.

Left bootie

LEG AND INSTEP

Foundation chain: Make 35[39:43]ch.

Row 1: 1dc in 2nd ch from hook, 1dc in each ch to end (34[38:42] sts).

Row 2: 1ch (does not count as st), 1dc in each ch to end (remembering to insert the hook into the back loop only of each st).

♥ ♥ ♥ Fabric-covered buttons are a great idea, as you can choose your own fabric to co-ordinate with the yarn and make a stylish statement. The button bases are available in a range of sizes and usually come with full instructions. You simply cut out a circle of fabric, stretch it over the top of the button, then press the button base in place, holding the fabric firmly and hiding the raw edges inside. ♥ ♥ ♥

Row 3: 1ch, 1dc in each dc to end.

Row 4: As row 3.

Row 5 (buttonhole): 1ch, 1dc in each dc to last 3dc, 2ch, miss 2dc, 1dc in last dc.

Row 6: 1ch, 1dc in each st to end.

Rep row 6 a further 4[6:8] times.

Next row (buttonhole): 1ch, 1dc in each dc to last 3dc, 2ch, miss 2dc, 1dc in last dc.

Rep row 6 a further 3 times.

Next row: Sl st in back loop only of 1st 8 sts, then work 1dc in each of next 18[22:26] sts, join last 8 sts and 1st 8 sts of row by working a sl st in each pair of sts, then work 1dc in each of last 2 sts; cut yarn and place a marker in last st worked (26[30:34] sts).

With WS facing, count back along row to 11th st from end and rejoin yarn to this st.

Next row: 1ch, 1dc in 1st st, 1dc in each of next 4 sts; turn.

Next row: 1ch, 1dc in 1st st, 1dc in each of next 7 sts; turn (8 sts).

Rep previous row 10[12:14] times. Cut yarn and fasten off.

Remove marker and rejoin yarn to this place, then with WS facing, work 1dc in each of next 10[12:14]dc, 11[13:15] sts evenly up side of instep, inserting hook into row ends, then 1dc in each of 8 sts along top, and 11[13:15]dc down opposite edge; turn.

Next row: 1ch, 1dc in each of next 23[27:31]dc, (dc2tog over next 2dc) twice, 1dc in each dc to end (48[56:64] sts).

Next row: 1ch, 1dc in each dc to end; turn.

Rep previous row a further 4[6:8] times. Cut yarn and fasten off.

Sole (make 2)

Foundation chain: Make 8[9:10]ch.

Row 1: 1dc in 2nd ch from hook, 1dc in each ch to end; turn (7[8:9] sts).

Row 2: 1ch, 2dc in first dc, 1dc in each of next 5[6:7]dc, 2dc in last dc; turn (9[11:13] sts).

Row 3: 1ch, 2dc in first dc, 1dc in each of next 7[8:9]dc, 2dc in last dc; turn (11[13:15] sts).

Row 4: 1ch, 1dc in each dc to end; turn.

Rep row 4 19[23:27] times.

Next row: 1ch, dc2tog over first 2dc, 1dc in each of next 7[8:9]dc, dc2tog over last 2dc (9[11:13] sts).

Next row: 1ch, dc2tog over first 2dc, 1dc in each of next 5[6:7]dc, dc2tog over last 2dc (7[9:11] sts).

Cut yarn and fasten off.

Making up

Stitch upper to sole.

Stitch buttons in place to correspond with buttonholes.

Baseball boots

Sporty and casual in style, these snug-fitting lace-ups are a move away from the more traditional bootie and are great for both baby boys and girls.

Size

To fit sizes 3–6[6–9:9–12] months
See size guide on pages 154–5

Tension

19 sts and 22 rows to 4in (10cm), measured over rows of double crochet using 3.50mm hook. Use a larger or smaller hook if necessary to obtain correct tension.

Materials and equipment

- 1 x 50g ball Artesano Soft Merino Superwash DK yarn in shade 0157 White (A)
- 1 x 50g ball Artesano Soft Merino Superwash DK yarn in shade SFN50 Black (B)
- Small amount of Artesano Superfine 100% Alpaca DK yarn in shade 0178 Peru (C)
- 3.50mm (UK9:USE-4) crochet hook
- Tapestry needle

20

Sole (make 2)

Foundation chain: Using yarn A, make 11[13:15]ch.

Round 1: 3dc in 2nd ch from hook, 1dc in each of next 8[10:12]ch, 6dc in last ch; then, working back along foundation chain, 1dc in each of next 8[10:12]ch, 3dc in last ch, join with sl st to 1st dc of round (28[32:36] sts).

Round 2: 1ch (does not count as st), 2dc in each of first 3dc, 1dc in each of next 8[10:12]dc, 2dc in each of next 6dc, 1dc in each of next 8[10:12]dc, 2dc in each of last 3dc; join with sl st to 1st dc of round (40[44:48] sts).

Round 3: 1ch, 2dc in 1st dc, 1dc in next dc, (2dc in next dc, 1dc in next dc) twice, 1dc in each of next 8[10:12]dc, (2dc in next dc, 1dc in next dc) 6 times, 1dc in each of next 8[10:12]dc, (2dc in next dc, 1dc in next dc) 3 times (52[56:60] sts).

Round 4: 1ch, 1dc in each dc of previous round. Fasten off.

Upper (make 2)

Foundation chain: Using yarn B, make 31[35:39]ch.

Row 1: 1dc in 2nd ch from hook, 1dc in each ch to end (30[34:38] sts).

Row 2: 1ch, 1dc in each dc of previous row. Rep row 2 a further 1[3:5] time(s).

Next row: 1ch, dc2tog over next 2dc, 1dc in each dc to last 2dc, dc2tog over last

2dc; turn. Rep previous row 3 times more (22[26:30] sts).

Next row: 1ch, 1dc in each dc of prev row.

EDGING

Round 1: 1ch, 1dc in 1st dc, 1dc in each of next 20[24:28]dc, 3dc in last dc of row, then 6[8:10]dc down sloping edge, 3[5:7]dc along straight edge, 3dc in 1st ch of foundation ch (place marker in 2nd of these 3dc), 1dc in each of next 28[32:36]ch, 3dc in last ch (place marker in 2nd of these 3dc), 3[5:7]dc along straight edge, 6[8:10]dc up opposite side, 2dc in same place as 1st dc of round (76[84:92] sts). Cut yarn B and fasten off.

Next row: Join yarn C to 1st marked st, then work 1ch, 1dc in each dc of previous row, finishing at 2nd marked st; fasten off.

Tongue (make 2)

Foundation chain: Using B, make 8[10:12]ch.

Row 1 (RS): 1dc in 2nd ch from hook, 1dc in each ch to end (7[9:11] sts).

Row 2: 1ch, 2dc in 1st dc, 1dc in each dc to last dc, 2dc in last dc (9[11:13] sts).

Row 3: 1ch, 1dc in each dc of previous row. Rep row 3 a further 9[11:13] times.

Next row: 1ch, 2dc in 1st dc, 1dc in each dc to last dc, 2dc in last dc (11[13:15] sts).

Row 14: 1ch, 1dc in each dc of previous row; turn.

EDGING

Round 1: 1ch, 1dc in each of first 10[12:14]

dc, 2dc in last dc of row, then 12[14:16] dc down side edge, 2dc in 1st ch of foundation ch, 1dc in each of next 5[7:9] ch, 2dc in last ch, 12[14:16]dc up opposite side, 1dc in same place as 1st dc of round, join with a sl st to 1st dc; fasten off (46[54:62] sts).

TOE CAP

Row 1: With RS facing, join yarn C to first dc of edging row and work 1ch, 1dc in same place, 1dc in each of next 10dc; fasten off (11[13:15] sts).

Row 2: With RS facing, miss first 2dc of row 1 and join yarn A to next dc, then work 1ch, miss next 2[3:4]dc and work 5dc[5htr:5tr] in next dc, miss next 2[3:4]dc and sl st into next dc; turn.

Row 3: 2dc in each of next 5 sts, miss next unworked dc and sl st into rem dc; turn.

Row 4: 1ch, (2dc in next dc, 1dc in next dc) 5 times, miss next unworked dc, sl st in last st (at end of row 1); do not turn and do not cut yarn.

JOIN TONGUE AND SOLE

Round 1: 1dc in each of next 2dc on side of tongue, then on lower edge of upper, insert hook through 1st dc and through next dc on side edge of tongue and work 2dc in same st to join; then working in lower edge of upper only, work 1dc in each of next 28[32:36] sts, then insert hook through last st and through 3rd dc from end of tongue edging and work 2dc,

then work 1dc in each of last 2dc on side edge of tongue, 1dc in row end on toe cap and 1dc in each dc around curved end of toe cap (52[56:60] sts).

Round 2: 1ch, 1dc in each dc of previous round; do not cut yarn A but join in C.

Round 3: Using C, 1ch, 1dc in each dc of previous round; cut C and fasten off.

Round 4: Using A, 1ch, 1dc in each dc of previous round.

JOIN SOLE AND UPPER

Pin centre back sole to centre back of upper.

Round 1: 1ch; then, inserting hook through one loop each of corresponding sts around edge of upper and edge of sole, work 1dc in each pair of sts to join. Fasten off.

Lace (make 2)

Using yarn A, make 95[100:105]ch; cut yarn and fasten off.

Disc (make 2)

Foundation chain: Using yarn A, make 4ch.

Round 1: 3ch, 11tr in ring, sl st in top of 3ch. Cut yarn and fasten off.

Making up

Use yarn ends to reinforce joins where corners of Upper meet edges of Toe Cap. Thread laces through gaps between stitches close to contrast edging on front. Stitch a disc to the outer side of each boot.

Frog face

These little pond-hoppers with funny smiley faces will delight your child. Knitted in bright green wool yarn, they are very eye-catching indeed.

Size

To fit sizes 0–6[6–12:12–18] months
See size guide on pages 154–5

Tension

24 sts and 36 rows to 4in (10cm), measured over stocking stitch, using 3mm needles. Use larger or smaller needles if necessary to obtain correct tension.

Materials and equipment

• 1 x 50g ball MillaMia Naturally Soft Merino yarn in shade 141 Grass (A)
• 1 x 50g ball MillaMia Naturally Soft Merino yarn in shade 124 Snow (B)
• Small amount of black 4-ply yarn
• 4 sew-on googly eyes
• 1 pair of 3mm (UK11:US2/3) knitting needles
• Stitch holder
• Tapestry needle

21

♥ ♥ ♥ This soft wool yarn is not a standard weight but falls somewhere between a 4-ply and DK. If you decide to substitute another yarn, it is essential that you check the tension. ♥ ♥ ♥

Main piece (make 2)

Using yarn A, cast on 37[41:45] sts.
Row 1 (RS): (K1, inc1, k15[17:19], inc1) twice, k1 (41[45:49] sts).
Row 2: Purl.
Row 3: (K1, inc1, k17[19:21], inc1) twice, k1 (45[49:53] sts).
Row 4: Purl.
Row 5: (K1, inc1, k19[21:23], inc1) twice, k1 (49[53:57] sts).
Beg with a purl row, work 7[9:11] rows in st st.

SHAPE FIRST SIDE OF ANKLE

Next row: K17[19:21]; turn and leave rem sts on a holder.
Next row: K1, p1, k1, purl to end.
Next row: K12[14:16], k2tog, k1, p1, k1 (16[18:20] sts).
Next row: K1, p1, k1, p2tog, p to end (15[17:19] sts).
Next row: K10[12:14], k2tog, k1, p1, k1 (14[16:18] sts).
Next row: K1, p1, k1, p2tog, p to end (13[15:17] sts).
Next row: K8[10:12], k2tog, k1, p1, k1 (12[14:16] sts).
Next row: (K1, p1) 6[7:8] times.
Next row (eyelet): *P1, k1; rep from * to last 4 sts, yfwd, k2tog, p1, k1.
Next row: (K1, p1) 6[7:8] times.
Cast off in pattern.

SHAPE SECOND SIDE OF ANKLE

With RS facing, leave the next 15 sts at centre on a holder and rejoin yarn to next st, then knit to end (17[19:21] sts).
Next row: P14[16:18], k1, p1, k1.
Next row: K1, p1, k1, sl1, k1, psso, k to end (16[18:20] sts).
Next row: P11[13:15], p2togtbl, k1, p1, k1 (15[17:19] sts).

Next row: K1, p1, k1, sl1, k1, psso, k to end (14[16:18] sts).
Next row: P9[11:13], p2togtbl, k1, p1, k1 (13[15:17] sts).
Next row: K1, p1, k1, sl1, k1, psso, k to end (12[14:16] sts).
Next row: (P1, k1) 6[7:8] times.
Next row (eyelet): K1, p1, k2tog, yfwd, (k1, p1) 4[5:6] times.
Next row: (P1, k1) 6[7:8] times.
Cast off in pattern.

INSTEP
Row 1 (RS): Cast on 6 sts, knit across sts on holder; turn (21 sts).
Row 2: Cast on 6 sts, p to end (27 sts).
Row 3: K16, sl1, k2tog, psso; turn.
Row 4: Sl1, p5, p3tog; turn.
Row 5: Sl1, k5, sl1, k2tog, psso; turn.
Rep rows 4 and 5 twice more, then row 4 once more (11 sts).
Row 11: Sl1, k to end.
Beg with a purl row, work 5 rows in st st.
Row 17: K1, (p1, k1) 5 times.
Rep row 17 twice more.
Cast off in pattern.

I-cord (make 2)
Using yarn A, cast on 80[85:90] sts.
Cast off, knitting each st tbl.

Eye (make 4)
Using yarn B, cast on 6 sts.
Row 1: Knit.
Row 2: Inc1 in each st (12 sts).
Row 3: Knit.
Row 4: Purl.
Row 5: Knit.
Row 6: (P2tog) 6 times.
Cut yarn and thread tail through rem 6 sts.

Making up
Fold shoe in half, with right sides together, and stitch seam along centre of sole and heel. Stitch cast-on stitches at each side of instep to inside of cuff at either side.

Stitch side edges of each eye piece together and pull up tail of yarn to close gap, then use same tail to stitch eyes in place. Stitch a googly plastic eye in the centre of each, or use black yarn to embroider eyes, as a safer alternative.

Thread tapestry needle with black yarn and embroider mouth in chain stitch (see page 137).

Thread cord through eyelet holes and tie in a bow.

Ladybird slippers

These cute slip-ons are knitted in red DK yarn; the black spots are crocheted separately and stitched in place. Add more or fewer spots as the fancy takes you.

Size

To fit sizes 0–6[6–12:12–18] months
See size guide on pages 154–5

Tension

24 sts and 36 rows to 4in (10cm), measured over stocking stitch, using 3mm needles. Use larger or smaller needles if necessary to obtain correct tension.

Materials and equipment

- 1 x 50g ball MillaMia Naturally Soft Merino yarn in shade 140 Scarlet
- 1 pair of size 3mm (UK11:US2/3) knitting needles
- Tapestry needle
- 6-stranded embroidery thread, in black
- 2.50mm (USB-1/C-2) crochet hook
- Shirring elastic, in red

22

♥ ♥ ♥ Shirring elastic threaded through the tops of these slippers helps to create a stretchy opening, ensuring a snug fit. ♥ ♥ ♥

Shoe (make 2)

Cast on 35[45:55] sts.

Row 1: Knit.

Row 2: K1, (m1, k16[21:26], m1, k1) twice (39[49:59] sts).

Row 3: Knit.

Row 4: K1, (m1, k18[23:28], m1, k1) twice (43[53:63] sts).

Row 5: Knit.

Row 6: K1, (m1, k20[25:30], m1, k1) twice (47[57:67] sts).

Row 7: Knit.

Row 8: K1, (m1, k22[27:32], m1, k1) twice (51[61:71] sts).

Row 9: Knit.

Row 10: K1, (m1, k24[29:34], m1, k1) twice (55[65:75] sts).

Row 11: Knit.

Row 12: Knit.

Row 13: Purl.

Rep rows 12 and 13 a further 2[3:4] times.

INSTEP

Row 1: K30[35:40], sl1, k1, psso, k1, turn.

Row 2: P7, p2tog, p1, turn.

Row 3: K8, sl1, k1, psso, k1, turn.

Row 4: P9, p2tog, p1, turn.

Row 5: K10, sl1, k1, psso, k1, turn.

Row 6: P11, p2tog, turn.

Row 7: K11, sl1, k1, psso, turn.

Rep rows 6 and 7 a further 6[7:8] times, then rep row 6 once more (35[43:51] sts).

Next row: Knit to end.

Knit 3 rows.

Cast off.

Spot (make 12)

Using 2.50mm crochet hook and black embroidery thread, make a magic loop (see page 151) and work 1ch (to secure ring), then 12dc into ring; join with a sl st to 1st dc, cut yarn, leaving a tail, and fasten off. Pull up tail of yarn to close hole in centre.

Making up

Fold shoe in half, with right sides together, and stitch back seam, then oversew seam along centre of sole. Weave in all yarn ends neatly. Turn right sides out.

Using tails of thread, securely stitch black spots to each shoe, in a symmetrical pattern.

Thread the tapestry needle with two strands of shirring elastic and thread in and out of stitches close to top edge of shoe. Pull up, not too tightly, knot ends together and then trim off excess.

Inuit boots

These chunky boots make great winter slippers for toddling around. Non-slip soles help to make them safer for babies who are a little unsteady on their feet.

Size

To fit sizes 12–15[15–18:18–24:24–36] months
See size guide on pages 154–5

Pattern note

Seam allowances are 1/4in (6mm) unless otherwise stated.

Pattern pieces

You will need the following pattern pieces from the pull-out sheet.
24 Upper • cut 2 in main fabric and 2 in lining fabric
25 Sole • cut 2 in main fabric and 2 in non-slip fabric

Materials and equipment

- Piece of 100% cotton medium-weight woven fabric, approximately 15^3/$_4$ x 23^1/$_2$in (40 x 60cm), in green, for main piece
- Piece of lightweight silk or polyester fabric, approximately 15^3/$_4$ x 23^1/$_2$in (40 x 60cm), in white, for lining
- Piece of non-slip fabric, approximately 6 x 4in (15 x 10cm), in red, for base of sole
- Sewing needle
- Sewing thread to match fabric
- 20in (50cm) of narrow elastic
- Approximately 63–71in (1.6–1.8m) of decorative braid, for ties
- 19^3/$_4$in (50cm) of ric-rac braid, for trim
- Sewing machine (optional)

23

1 Cut two uppers from both main fabric and lining, and two soles from both main fabric and non-slip fabric using the list on page 98 and the pull-out sheet. Put the sole pieces to one side. With right sides together, stitch straight edges of leg and leg lining together.

2 Cut two pieces of elastic, each 8[8¼:8½:9]in 20[21:22:23]cm long. Stitch one piece of elastic to the wrong side of each main piece, referring to the pattern template for positioning. You will need to attach each end of the elastic to the fabric at either side, then stretch the elastic as you stitch.

3 Cut the braid into four equal lengths, at least 15¾in (40cm) long (or slightly longer for the larger sizes). Take two lengths and pin, then baste the ends to the back seam allowance where indicated on the pattern template. With right sides together, stitch the back seam, trapping the ends of the braid firmly in place.

4 Turn the leg section right sides out and pin, then baste the lower edge of the lining and the lower edge of the main fabric together, within the seam allowance.

5 With wrong sides together, baste the fabric sole and the non-slip sole together, for each slipper.

6 Pin, then baste the sole to the upper on each slipper, with the seam allowance on the outside. Stitch inside the seam allowance.

7 Use bias binding to bind the seam allowance all around the base, starting and ending at centre back of sole.

8 For a neat finishing touch, stitch ric-rac braid around the top edge of the leg on each slipper, starting and finishing at the back seam.

❤ ❤ ❤ **A medium-weight woven cotton fabric is a good choice for these substantial slippers; check the remnants bin in the furnishing fabrics department of your favourite fabric shop. Alternatively, you could use velvet, needlecord or tweed.** ❤ ❤ ❤

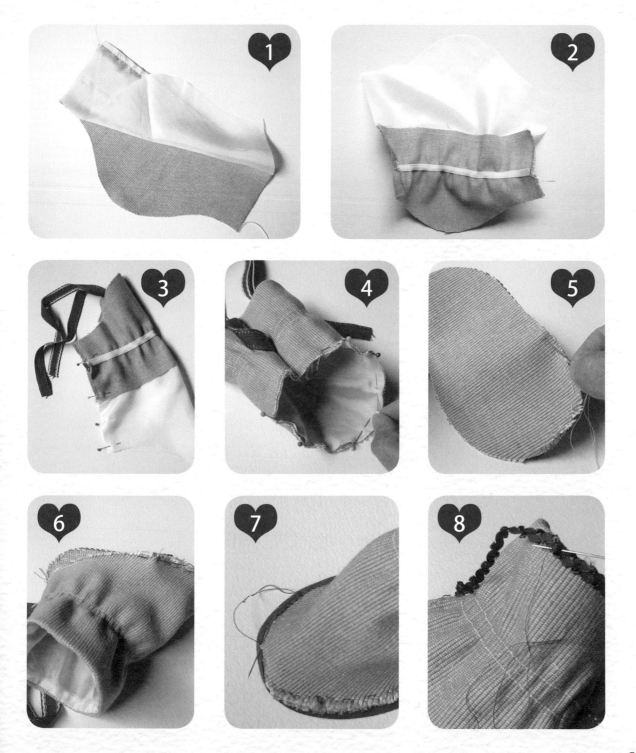

Inuit boots

Jungle print

Your little explorer can walk on the wild side in these stylish slippers. The combination of a soft elastic edge and a drawstring fastening will help to keep them in place.

Size

To fit sizes 6–9[9–12:12–15:15–18] months
See size guide on pages 154–5

Pattern note

Seam allowances are ¼in (6mm) unless otherwise stated.

Pattern pieces

You will need the following pattern pieces from the pull-out sheet.

26 Back · cut 2 in main fabric and 2 in lining
27 Toe · cut 2 in main fabric and 2 in lining
28 Sole · cut 2 in main fabric, 2 in lining and 2 in interfacing

Materials and equipment

- Piece of faux fur or fleece fabric, approximately 15¾ x 12in (40 x 30cm), in leopard print
- Piece of 100% cotton lawn, approximately 15¾ x 12in (40 x 30cm), in pink, for lining
- Piece of medium-weight non-fusible interfacing, approximately 6 x 4in (15 x 10cm)
- Sewing needle
- Sewing thread to match fabric
- 59in (1.5m) of 1in (25mm) bias binding
- 16in (40cm) of cord elastic
- 36in (90cm) of narrow gold ribbon
- Sewing machine (optional)

24

1 Using the templates listed on page 102 from the pull-out sheet, cut two toe pieces, two back pieces and two soles from both the main fabric and the lining, and two soles from interfacing. Sandwich the interfacing between the main fabric and lining to form the soles, then pin and baste.

2 Stitch through all three layers within the seam allowance, then trim away excess interfacing all round to reduce the bulk.

3 For the toe section, place main fabric and lining together, wrong sides out, and stitch seam on the shorter of the two curved edges. Turn right sides out and

press, then topstitch approximately $1/4$in (6mm) from the edge to form a casing. Cut the elastic into two equal lengths and insert one into each toe section. Pull up to gather, stitch through fabric at either end of casing to secure elastic in place, then trim off excess elastic and discard.

4 For the back section, neaten the pointed ends of both main fabric and lining pieces by turning $3/16$in (5mm) to wrong side and stitch to form a single narrow hem. Place main fabric and lining together, wrong sides out, and stitch seam on shorter of the two curved edges. Turn right sides out and press, then topstitch approximately $1/4$in (6mm) from the edge to form a casing.

5 With wrong sides out, pin the toe sections to the soles (so the seam will be on the inside). Then position each back piece, lining up the centre of each back to the centre back of each sole, and overlapping the corners over the toe pieces. Pin, baste and then stitch.

6 On the pointed ends of the back pieces, oversew edges of main fabric and lining together, then cut the gold ribbon into two equal lengths and thread through top casings.

Baby Booties and Slippers

♥ ♥ ♥ Faux fur fabric is available in a range of different animal prints; choose a fabric with a short, soft, velvety pile, then select a bright-coloured cotton lawn – or a silk or polyester lining fabric, if you prefer – to make an eye-catching contrast lining. ♥ ♥ ♥

Winter warmers

Knitted in pure soft merino wool, with a snug fit and foldover cuff, these booties are guaranteed to keep precious little feet warm all winter long.

Size

To fit sizes 3–6[6–9:9–12] months
See size guide on pages 154–5

Tension

24 sts and 36 rows to 4in (10cm), measured over stocking stitch, using 3.25mm needles. Use larger or smaller needles if necessary to obtain correct tension.

Materials and equipment

• 1 x 50g ball Debbie Bliss Rialto DK yarn in shade 44 Aqua
• 1 pair of 3.25mm (UK10:US3) needles
• Tapestry needle

25

Shoe (make 2)

Cast on 25[33:41] sts.

Row 1: Inc1, k10[14:18], inc1, k1, inc1, k10[14:18], inc1 (29[37:45] sts).

Row 2: Inc1, p12[16:20], inc1, p1, inc1, p12[16:20], inc1 (33[41:49] sts).

Row 3: Inc1, k14[18:22], inc1, k1, inc1, k14[18:22], inc1 (37[45:53] sts).

Row 4: Inc1, p16[20:24], inc1, p1, inc1, p16[20:24], inc1 (41[49:57] sts).

Row 5: Inc1, k18[22:26], inc1, k1, inc1, k18[22:26], inc1 (45[53:61] sts).

Row 6: Inc1, p20[24:30], inc1, p1, inc1, p20[24:30], inc1 (49[57:65] sts).

Row 7: P2tog, p to end (48[56:64] sts).

Beg with a purl row, work 3 rows in st st.

Knit 10[12:14] rows.

INSTEP

Row 1: K22[26:30], k2tog, k2tog tbl, k22[26:30] (46[54:62] sts).

Row 2: P21[25:29], p2tog tbl, p2tog, p21[25:29] (44[52:60] sts).

Row 3: K20[24:28], k2tog, k2tog tbl, k20[24:28] (42[50:58] sts).

Row 4: P19[23:27], p2tog tbl, p2tog, p19[23:27] (40[48:56] sts).

Row 5: K18[22:26], k2tog, k2tog tbl, k18[22:26] (38[46:54] sts).

Row 6: P17[21:25], p2tog tbl, p2tog, p17[21:25] (36[44:52] sts).

Row 7: K16[20:24], k2tog, k2tog tbl, k16[20:24] (34[42:50] sts).

SIZES 6–9 MONTHS AND 9–12 MONTHS ONLY:

Row 8: P[19:23], p2tog tbl, p2tog, p[19:23] ([40:48] sts).

Row 9: K[18:22], k2tog, k2tog tbl, k[18:22] ([38:46] sts).

SIZE 9–12 MONTHS ONLY:

Row 10: P21, p2tog tbl, p2tog, p21 (44 sts).

ALL SIZES:

Next row: *K1, p1; rep from * to end.

Rep previous row a further 6[8:11] times more.

Beg with a knit row, work 6 rows in st st.

Knit 14[16:18] rows.

Cast off.

Making up

Fold bootie in half, with right sides together, and stitch the seam along the centre of the sole by oversewing or grafting together stitches on cast-on edge. Stitch the back seam, reversing the seam on the garter-stitch band at the top of the leg, so that the seam is on the inside when the cuff is folded over.

♥ ♥ ♥ The band of ribbing on the leg helps the bootie to fit snugly around the ankle so it is less likely to slip off. If you wish, you can make it fit more tightly by running one or two lengths of shirring elastic through these stitches. ♥ ♥ ♥

Fresh blossom

Embellished with hand-embroidered flowers, these are special-occasion shoes that are too nice to save for best – and are actually practical enough to wear every day.

Size

To fit sizes 6–9[9–12:12–15:15–18] months. See size guide on pages 154–5

Pattern note

Seam allowances are $1/4$in (6mm) unless otherwise stated.

Pattern pieces

You will need the following pattern pieces from the pull-out sheet.

29 **Upper** • cut 2 in waffle fabric and 2 in lining fabric

30 **Sole** • cut 2 in waffle fabric and 2 in lining fabric

31 **Embroidery motif**

Materials and equipment

- Piece of 100% cotton waffle fabric, approximately $15^3/_4$ x 12in (40 x 30cm), in white, for main piece
- Piece of 100% cotton lawn fabric, approximately $15^3/_4$ x 12in (40 x 30cm), in pale yellow, for lining
- Crewel needle
- 6-stranded embroidery thread, in yellow, pink, green and blue
- Embroidery hoop
- Sewing needle
- Sewing thread, in white
- 36in (90cm) of cotton tape or ribbon, in white
- Sewing machine (optional)

26

1 Trace the pattern pieces listed on page 110 from the pull-out sheet on to tracing paper and cut out to make templates (see page 134). Place the template for the upper on to the white waffle fabric and draw around it twice, but do not cut them out yet. Trace the embroidery motif on to thin paper, using a transfer pen or pencil, then place this in position on the fabric and press with a hot iron to transfer the design on to the fabric. Place the fabric in an embroidery hoop and fill in the shapes in satin stitch (see page 135) using two strands of thread.

2 Once the embroidery is complete, remove the fabric from the hoop and press on the wrong side, then cut out the fabric shapes.

3 Place the two short straight edges of the upper together and stitch to form back seam (seam is on inside of shoe). Press the back seam of the shoe open. Do this for the two main pieces and the two lining pieces.

4 Pin, baste and stitch the upper part of the main fabric to the sole piece and snip curves. Do the same with the lining for both shoes. Snip into the seam allowance at the front of each shoe, around the curves.

5 Turn the main part of each shoe right sides out, then place the linings inside the shoes. Turn under $3/16$in (5mm) on the top edge of both lining and shoe, and baste.

6 Slipstitch top edges of main fabric and lining together using small, neat stitches. Leave the back part of each shoe open at this stage.

7 Cut the tape or ribbon into two equal lengths, then stitch the centre of the tape to the inside back seam on each shoe. Turn under $3/16$in (5mm) on both main fabric and lining and oversew edges together.

8 Tie the ends of the tapes in a neat bow at the front of each shoe, then trim ends diagonally to prevent fraying.

♥ ♥ ♥ **Remember that soft shoes like this, made entirely from fabric, offer no support for tiny feet; they are designed to be worn as pram shoes, and not for walking.** ♥ ♥ ♥

Baby Booties and Slippers

Ankle tie

These two-colour shoes in soft alpaca yarn with crossover fronts, ankle ties and pretty flower embellishments are perfect for special occasions.

Size

To fit sizes 9–12 [12–15:15–18] months
See size guide on pages 154–5

Tension

22 sts and 34 rows to 4in (10cm), measured over rows of double crochet using 3.50mm hook. Use a larger or smaller hook if necessary to obtain correct tension.

Pattern pieces

You will need the following pattern pieces from the pull-out sheet.

32 **Sole** • cut 2 in soft leather

Materials and equipment

- 1 x 50g ball Artesano 4-ply 100% Alpaca yarn in shade CA13 Sweet Pea (A)
- 1 x 50g ball Artesano 4-ply 100% Alpaca yarn in shade C726 Amarylis (B)
- Small amounts of 4-ply cotton yarn in green, yellow and pink
- 3.50mm (UK9:USE-4) crochet hook
- 2.50mm (UK12:USB-1/C-2) crochet hook
- Tapestry needle
- Offcut of soft leather, approximately 6in (15cm) square
- Leather punch

27

♥ ♥ ♥ This is quite a complex pattern, as it has a number of different elements. Each side is worked separately, in a different coloured yarn, and the sloped edges at the front of each piece, created by increasing stitches on each row, have to be wrapped around and sewn in place, forming a double layer of fabric at the toe. There is also a border and ankle ties to be worked, as well as the flower embellishment. As work progresses, you will find it helpful to refer to the picture of the finished shoes to understand how each one is constructed. ♥ ♥ ♥

Sole (make 2)

Using template listed on page 114 from pull-out sheet, cut two soles from soft leather and punch holes, as indicated on the pattern pieces.

Left shoe

FIRST (LEFT-HAND) SIDE

Foundation round: Using 3.50mm crochet hook and yarn A, with WS of sole facing, join yarn to hole at centre back of sole and work 1ch (does not count as st), 1dc in same place, then 2dc in each of next 10[12:14] holes, 3dc in each of next 2 holes, 1dc in next hole; turn (28[32:36] sts).
Row 1: 1ch, 2dc in 1st dc, 1dc in each dc to end of row; turn.

Row 2: 1ch, 1dc in 1st dc, 1dc in each dc to last dc, 2dc in last dc; turn.
Rep rows 1 and 2 a further 4[5:6] times (38[44:50] sts).
Fasten off, leaving a tail of yarn for sewing up.

SECOND (RIGHT-HAND) SIDE

With RS (underside) of sole facing, join yarn B to centre back hole.
Foundation row: 1ch, 1dc in same hole, 2dc in each of next 9[11:13] holes, 1dc in same hole as 1dc in yarn A, then 1dc in each of next 8dc, at back of work, inserting hook around post of each st; turn (28[32:36] sts).
Row 1: 1ch, 2dc in 1st dc, 1dc in each dc to end of row; turn.
Row 2: 1ch, 1dc in 1st dc, 1dc in each dc to last dc, 2dc in last dc; turn.
Rep rows 1 and 2 a further 4[5:6] times (38[44:50] sts).
Fasten off, leaving a tail of yarn for sewing up.

Right shoe

For right shoe, follow instructions for left shoe but for first side (which will be the right-hand side), begin with RS of sole facing; then for second side, in yarn B, when you get to the toe work into stitches at the front of the work.

Making up

Stitch back seam on each shoe. On the outside, stitch sloping edge of side worked in yarn B to stitches in yarn A along edge of sole. On the inside, stitch sloping edge worked in yarn A to stitches in B on inside edge of sole. Then stitch straight edges in place on the inside and outside.

Border (both shoes)

Rejoin A to top of centre back seam then with RS facing, work 1ch.

Round 1: 1dc in each of first 2dc, dc2tog over next 2dc, 1dc in each of next 19[23:27]dc, (dc2tog) twice, then holding edges of both sides together where they overlap at centre front, inserting hook through both layers, work (1dc in next dc) twice, then working through single layer work (dc2tog) twice, 1dc in each of next 19[23:27]dc, dc2tog over next 2dc, 1dc in each of last 2dc; join with sl st to 1st dc of round (54[58:62] sts).

Round 2: 1ch, 1dc in each of first 2dc, dc2tog over next 2dc, 1dc in each of next 17[21:25]dc, htr4tog over next 4dc, 1dc in each of next 17[21:25]dc, dc2tog over next 2dc, 1dc in each of last 2dc; join with sl st to 1st dc of round; fasten off.

Tie (both shoes)

Row 1: Using 3.50mm hook and yarn A, make 48ch, then work 1sl st into each of 4[6:8]dc of border at centre back of shoe, then 49ch; turn.

Row 2: 1dc in 2nd ch from hook, then 1dc into each ch and sl st of previous row; fasten off.

Leaf (make 4)

Using 2.50mm hook and green yarn, make 6ch.

Round 1: 1dc in 2nd ch from hook, 1htr in each of next 2ch, 1tr in next ch, 3tr in last ch; then, working along opposite edge of foundation ch, 1tr in next ch, 1htr in each of next 2ch, 1dc in next ch, sl st into last ch; fasten off, leaving a tail of yarn.

Flower (make 2)

Using 2.50mm hook and yellow yarn, make a magic loop.

Round 1: 1ch, 10dc in ring join with sl st to 1st dc of round; fasten off and join in pink yarn.

Round 2: 1ch, *(1tr, 2dtr, 1tr) in next ch, 1dc in next ch, rep from * 4 times more, working last dc into 1st ch of round; fasten off, leaving a tail of yarn.

To finish

Stitch a pair of leaves to the centre front of each shoe, along the border, then stitch a flower in the centre of each pair of leaves.

Stripy booties

The unusual structure of these snug booties with their snazzy stripes makes them fun and different to make – and even more fun to wear.

Size

To fit sizes 3–6[6–9:9–12] months
See size guide on pages 154–5

Tension

24 sts and 36 rows to 4in (10cm), measured over stocking stitch, using 3.25mm needles. Use larger or smaller needles if necessary to obtain correct tension.

Materials and equipment

- 1 x 50g ball MillaMia Naturally Soft Merino yarn in shade 101 Midnight (A)
- 1 x 50g ball MillaMia Naturally Soft Merino yarn in shade 144 Peacock (B)
- 1 pair of 3.25mm (UK10:US3) needles
- Tapestry needle
- 39½in (1m) narrow ribbon

28

Upper (make 2)

Using yarn A, cast on 18[20:22] sts; do not cut A but join in B.

Row 1: Using B, k7[8:9]; turn.

Row 2: Purl to end.

Row 3: Using A, knit to end.

Row 4: Purl to end.

Rep rows 1–4 a further 2[3:4] times more.

Next row: Using B, inc1, k6[7:8]; turn.

Next row: Purl to end.

Next row: Using A, knit to end.

Next row: Purl to end.

Next row: Using B, inc1, k7[8:9]; turn.

Next row: Purl to end.

Next row: Using A, knit to end.

Next row: Purl to end.

Next row: Using B, inc1, k8[9:10]; turn.

Next row: Purl to end.

Next row: Using A, knit to end.

Next row: Purl to end.

Next row: Using B, inc1, k9[10:11]; turn.

Next row: Purl to end.

Next row: Using A, knit to end.

Next row: Purl to end.

Next row: Using B, inc1, k10[11:12]; turn.

Next row: Purl to end.

Next row: Using A, knit to end.

Next row: Purl to end.

Next row: Using B, inc1, k11[12:13]; turn.

Next row: Purl to end.

Next row: Using A, knit to end.

Next row: Purl to end.

***Next row:** Using B, k13[14:15]; turn.

Next row: Purl to end.

Next row: Using A, knit to end.

Next row: Purl to end. *

Rep from * to * 2[3:4] times.

Next row: Using B, k2tog, k11[12:13]; turn.

Next row: Purl to end.

Next row: Using A, knit to end.

Next row: Purl to end.

Next row: Using B, k2tog, k10[11:11]; turn.

Next row: Purl to end.

Next row: Using A, knit to end.

Next row: Purl to end.

Next row: Using B, k2tog, k9[10:11]; turn.

Next row: Purl to end.

Next row: Using A, knit to end.

Next row: Purl to end.

Next row: Using B, k2tog, k8[9:10]; turn.

Next row: Purl to end.

Next row: Using A, knit to end.

Next row: Purl to end.

Next row: Using B, k2tog, k7[8:9]; turn.

Next row: Purl to end.

Next row: Using A, knit to end.

Next row: Purl to end.

Next row: Using B, k2tog, k6[7:8]; turn.

Next row: Purl to end.

****Next row:** Using A, knit to end.

Next row: Purl to end.

Next row: Using B, k7[8:9]; turn.

Next row: Purl to end. **

Rep from ** to ** 2[3:4] times more.

Cast off using A.

Sole (make 2)

Using yarn A, cast on 7[8:9] sts.

Rows 1 and 2: Knit.

Row 3: Inc1, k5[6:7], inc1 (9[10:11] sts).
Knit 35[39:43] rows.

Next row: K2tog, k to last 2 sts, k2tog
(7[8:9] sts).

Next row: Knit.

Cast off.

Making up

Stitch the back seam, reversing the seam on
the top half of the plain band that forms the
leg so that the seam is on the inside when
the cuff is folded over.

Stitch the sole to the upper, matching centre
fronts and centre backs on both pieces.

Cut the ribbon in half and, beginning at
the pair of holes at centre front formed
by the turning rows, thread one 19¾in
(50cm) length through eyelets on each
shoe and tie ends in a neat bow.

💜 🖤 💜 Short rows help to shape
the shoe as well as creating the smart
stripes. Although the pattern may seem
a little tricky when you first read through
it, these delightful booties are actually
very straightforward and quick to make as
long as you follow the directions carefully.
Use your own favourite colour combination
for an eye-catching result. 💜 🖤 💜

Teddy bear

Soft and snug, with a pair of friendly teddy-bear faces, these alpaca slippers are not only warm but make fun little characters to talk to and play with.

Size

To fit sizes 6–9 [9–12:12–15] months
See size guide on pages 154–5

Tension

20 sts and 22 rows to 4in (10cm), measured over rows of double crochet, using 3.50mm hook. Use a larger or smaller hook if necessary to obtain correct tension.

Materials and equipment

- 1 x 50g ball Artesano 100% Alpaca yarn in shade NZ95 Caramel Twist (A)
- 1 x 50g ball Artesano 100% Alpaca yarn in shade SFN10 Cream (B)
- Small amount of DK or tapestry yarn in black
- 3.50mm (UK9:USE-4) crochet hook
- Stitch marker
- Tapestry needle
- 2 domed buttons with shank, black
- 4 small, round, flat buttons, black
- Sewing needle
- Black sewing thread

29

Slipper (make 2)

Foundation chain: Using yarn A, make 36[40:44]ch.

Foundation row: 1dc in 2nd ch from hook, 1dc in each ch to end (35[39:43] sts).

Row 1: 1ch (does not count as st), 1dc in 1st dc, (1ch, miss 1dc, 1dc in next dc) 17[19:21] times.

Row 2: 1ch, 1dc in each dc and 1-ch sp to end.

Row 3: 1ch, 1dc in 1st dc, 1dc in each of next 22[25:28]dc; turn.

Row 4: 1ch, 1dc in 1st dc, 1dc in each of next 10[12:14]dc; turn and place marker in base of last st worked.

INSTEP

Work 8[10:12] rows of dc on these centre 11[13:15] sts; cut yarn and fasten off.

UPPER

Row 1: With RS facing, rejoin yarn to marked st and work 1ch then 8[10:12]dc along side of instep, 1dc in each dc along top, 8[10:12]dc down opposite side and 1dc in each dc to end.

Row 2: 1ch, 1dc in each dc to end (51[59:67] sts).

Rep row 2 a further 6[8:10] times.

SOLE

Row 1: 1ch, 1dc in 1st dc, (dc2tog over next 2dc, 1dc in each of next 20[24:28] dc, dc2tog over next 2dc, 1dc in next dc) twice (47[55:63] sts).

Row 2: 1ch, 1dc in 1st dc, (dc2tog over next 2dc, 1dc in each of next 18[22:26] dc, dc2tog over next 2dc, 1dc in next dc) twice (43[51:59] sts).

Row 3: 1ch, 1dc in 1st dc, (dc2tog over next 2dc, 1dc in each of next 16[20:24] dc, dc2tog over next 2dc, 1dc in next dc) twice (39[47:55] sts).

Row 4: 1ch, 1dc in 1st dc, (dc2tog over next 2dc, 1dc in each of next 14[18:22] dc, dc2tog over next 2dc, 1dc in next dc) twice (35[42:51] sts).

Row 5: 1ch, 1dc in 1st dc, (dc2tog over next 2dc, 1dc in each of next 12[16:20] dc, dc2tog over next 2dc, 1dc in next dc) twice; cut yarn and fasten off.

Making up

Stitch underfoot and back seams. Starting at centre back, thread a tie cord through eyelet holes just below top edge of each shoe.

Face (make 2)

Using yarn B, make a magic loop and work 1ch (to secure ring), then 9dc into ring; join with a sl st to 1st dc and pull up tail of yarn to close hole in centre.

Round 1: 1ch, 2dc in each dc of previous round (18 sts).

Round 2: 1ch, 1dc in 1st dc, 2dc in next dc, (1dc in next dc, 2dc in next dc) 8 times (27 sts).

Round 3: 1ch, 1dc in each dc of previous round.

Round 4: 1ch, 1dc in each of first 2dc, 2dc in next dc, (1dc in each of next 2dc, 2dc in next dc) 8 times; cut yarn and fasten off, leaving a tail of yarn.

Ear (make 4)

Using yarn B, make a magic loop and work 1ch (to secure ring), then 9dc into ring; join with a sl st to 1st dc and pull up tail of yarn to close hole in centre.

Row 1: 1ch, 1dc in 1st st, 2dc in each of next 6 sts, 1dc in next st; cut yarn and fasten off.

Row 2: Join A to 1st dc of previous round and work 1ch, 1dc in each dc of previous round; cut yarn and fasten off.

Cord (make 2)

Using yarn A, make 65ch and work 1sl st in 2nd ch from hook then 1sl st in each ch to end; cut yarn and fasten off.

🖤 🖤 🖤 **Buttons must be attached securely; if you prefer, you could embroider the bear's features instead, using black yarn.** 🖤 🖤 🖤

To finish

Stitch the face firmly to the front of the slipper by oversewing the edges, stitch by stitch, using the tail of yarn, then stitch two ears to edges of face, oversewing the lower edge of each ear to the edge of the face. Weave in remaining yarn ends. Insert the shank of the button into the central hole on the face and stitch securely in place on the inside of the shoe. Stitch on two small black buttons for eyes. Thread the tapestry needle with a length of black yarn and embroider the mouth: one straight stitch going down from the base of the nose and a curved line of backstitch following the lines of the crocheted stitches. Thread the cord through the eyelet holes on each slipper, starting and ending at centre back, then tie the ends in a bow.

Colourful cupcakes

Made in bright and cheerful sugar-candy colours, these comfortable and cosy little slippers almost look good enough to eat.

Size

To fit size 0–3[3–6:6–9] months
See size guide on pages 154–5

Tension

25 sts and 32 rows to to 4in (10cm), measured over stocking stitch, using 3mm needles. Use larger or smaller needles if necessary to obtain correct tension.

Materials and equipment

- 1 x 50g ball Anchor Style Creativa Fino 100% cotton 4-ply in 0295 Citron (A)
- 1 x 50g ball Anchor Style Creativa Fino 100% cotton 4-ply in 1320 Pink (B)
- 1 x 50g ball Anchor Style Creativa Fino 100% cotton 4-ply in 1338 Orange (C)
- 1 x 50g ball Anchor Style Creativa Fino 100% cotton 4-ply in 1330 Apple Green (D)
- 1 pair of 3mm (UK11:US2/3) knitting needles
- Tapestry needle

30

Slipper (make 2)

Using yarn A, cast on 40[48:56] sts.
Row 1: Knit.
Row 2: K2, m1, k3, m1, k30[38:46], m1, k3, m1, k2 (44[52:60] sts).
Row 3: Knit.
Row 4: K2, m1, k3, m1, k34[42:50], m1, k3, m1, k2 (48[56:64] sts).
Knit 3 rows.
Row 8: K21[25:29], (k1, m1) 6 times, k21[25:29] (54[62:70] sts).
Row 9: P2[2:0], *k1, p2; rep from * to last 1[0:1] st, k1[0:1].
Row 10: P1[0:1], *k2, p1; rep from * to last 2[2:0] sts, k2[2:0].
Rep rows 9 and 10 a further 4[5:6] times.
Next row: K15[19:23], (k2tog) 12 times, k15[19:23] (42[50:58] sts).
Next row: Purl.
Next row: K13[17:21], (k2tog) 8 times, k13[17:21] (34[42:50] sts).
Next row: Purl.
Knit 2 rows.
Cast off.

Topper (make 2)

Using yarn B, cast on 6 sts.
Row 1: K1, (m1, k1) 5 times (11 sts).
Row 2: Purl.
Row 3: K1, (m1, k1) 10 times (21 sts).
Row 4: Purl.
Row 5: (M1, k2) 10 times, k1 (31 sts).
Row 6: Purl.

Row 7: K2, (m1, k3) 9 times, m1, k2 (41 sts).
Row 8: Knit.
Cast off.

Petal (make 2)

Using yarn C, cast on 7 sts.
Row 1: Knit each st tbl.
Row 2: Purl.
Row 3: Cast off 4 sts, k to end (3 sts).
Row 4: K3, turn and cast on 4 sts (7 sts).
Rep rows 1–4 a further 3 times, then rows 1–3 once; cast off rem sts.
Fasten off, leaving a tail of yarn.

Spiral (make 2)

Using yarn D, cast on 12 sts.
Row 1: Purl.
Row 2: Inc1 in each st (24 sts).
Cast off.
Fasten off, leaving a tail of yarn.

Making up

Fold slipper in half, with right sides together, and stitch back seam; then oversew seam along centre of sole. Turn right sides out.

💜 🖤 💜 **You can use any standard 4-ply cotton yarn for this project, making sure before you begin that it knits to the tension stated in the pattern.** 🖤 🖤 🖤

At centre front opening of each slipper, pinch the edges of the garter-stitch border together and stitch to form a small ridge about ³/₈in (10mm) long.

Pin one topper to the top of each slipper, with the centre of the circle at the front of the small ridge, and the two straight edges just below the garter-stitch border of the slipper on either side. Stitch in place along the border, but leave the curved outer edge of the topper unstitched.

To make up the flower, join the row of petals into a ring by stitching the cast-on and cast-off edges together; then sew a running stitch around the base of the petals and pull up to gather and close up the gap in the centre. Stitch one flower to each slipper, on top of the small ridge at the centre front.

Coil up the spiral quite tightly, stitching through the cast-on edge, then stitch one spiral to the centre of each flower.

TECHNIQUES

Sewing techniques

These quick little projects are a great way to brush up your sewing skills, while the many methods of embellishing the booties will give an outlet to your creativity.

Tools and materials

All the sewn booties in this book are easy to make, requiring only the most basic equipment and skills. If you have a sewing machine, you may find it useful for some of the processes, but you should be able to complete all of the projects by hand.

Fabrics

Think of your baby's feet when choosing fabrics and try to select something smooth and breathable. Cotton fabrics have a nicer feel than poly-cotton blends and they are available in a dazzling array of plain colours, stripes, checks and prints. Linen is another natural fabric that is crisp and cool; linen or a linen-cotton blend can be used for most of the sewn shoes in this book. The little embroidered shoes on page 110 have been made from waffle cotton; this has a lovely texture, although any cotton or linen fabric could be used instead. Before cutting and stitching, it is advisable to wash new cotton and linen fabrics, as they may shrink; it is better to pre-shrink them than for your baby shoes to come out of the washing machine smaller than when they went in.

Two of the projects use felt: it is important to choose felt fabric made from wool or a wool blend rather than craft felt of the kind sold in craft and hobby shops, as the latter is neither hard-wearing nor washable.

For shoes that require lining, choose a fine cotton such as lawn, or a silk lining such as habutai.

Thread

As a general rule, whether sewing by hand or machine, choose a thread with a fibre content that matches the fabric: so for cotton fabrics, use cotton thread.

Try to match the colour of the fabric as closely as possible; if an exact match is not possible, choose a slightly darker shade.

Embellishments

Adding decorative details such as lace, braid, ribbon, buttons and bows can turn a simple shoe into a minor work of art. Make sure that all trims are well secured and think twice before attaching buttons to shoes if there is any danger that they might be pulled off and swallowed by your baby.

Pins and needles

Use dressmakers' pins to pin pattern pieces to fabric and to hold fabric pieces together before sewing. Those with glass heads are most useful as they are easy to handle and easy to see. They are also useful for knitting and crochet projects, where the heads are less likely to get lost amid the folds of the fabric.

Sewing machine

Although it is not necessary to use a sewing machine on very small projects like these booties and slippers, a sewing machine will produce stronger seams than you can achieve by hand and can speed up the sewing process.

Other tools

♥ Scissors are essential items. Keep the ones you use for cutting fabrics separate, as using them to cut other materials will make them blunt. Choose dressmaking shears for cutting fabric; a pair of small, sharp, pointed embroidery scissors for snipping thread and unpicking; and a pair of all-purpose scissors for general use.

♥ A ruler is useful for measuring and marking straight lines. A tape measure is essential for measuring contours.

♥ An iron is essential for smoothing out fabric before cutting and for pressing seams as you work to produce a neat finish.

♥ An embroidery hoop is very useful for keeping fabric taut while stitching.

Safety note

Because you are making these little shoes for very small children and babies, it is vital that you use safe, clean, new materials. Also, think twice before stitching googly eyes and buttons to slippers intended for a very young child if he or she is likely to pull them off; you may prefer to embroider eyes instead, or use another method of fastening.

Basic sewing techniques

The sewn booties featured in this book require only basic sewing skills to construct the projects.

Pattern pieces

To make a template, select the correct size pattern piece and either trace it using tracing paper and a pencil, or photocopy it. You can either pin your tracing or copy on to the fabric and cut along the lines, through both paper and fabric, or you can stick the tracing or copy on to thin card, cut it out, then place the card shape on to the fabric and draw around it, then cut out the fabric shape.

Sewing a seam

Pin pieces together, then baste (see below) and stitch by hand or machine, 1/4in (6mm) from the edges. Sewing a curved seam by hand is easy, but with a sewing machine you will need to do this more slowly, easing the fabric carefully as you stitch. After sewing a curved seam, snip into the fabric at right angles to the stitch line, at intervals of about 1/4in (6mm); this helps to prevent the fabric from puckering and produces a smoother line when the item is turned right sides out. **(A)**

Basting

Basting (tacking) fabrics together before sewing helps them to stay in place. Use a long running stitch for basting and remove it after the sewing is complete and before pressing. **(B)**

A

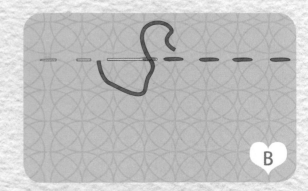

B

Hand stitches

Hand stitches can be both functional, used in the construction of a piece, or decorative, used as embellishment once the bootie has been put together. Backstitch, explained on page 144, is also used frequently for hand-sewing seams or as a decorative stitch.

Running stitch

The simplest of hand stitches, this stitch is used to gather a piece of fabric, to baste fabric pieces together (using a longer stitch length, sometimes referred to as a 'tacking' stitch), and as a decorative stitch using embroidery thread. Bring the needle up through the fabric to the right side, then, working from right to left, push the needle tip in and out of the fabric several times, at equal intervals. **(C)**

Slipstitch

Sometimes referred to as 'oversewing', this stitch is usually used for appliqué, for hemming or to join two folded edges; for example, when sewing a lining to a shoe. If you keep your stitches small it will produce a neat, almost invisible result. Use the needle tip to pick up a few threads from both fabrics at short intervals, working from right to left. **(D)**

Satin stitch

Use this filling-in stitch for the embroidered flowers on page 110. Bring the needle to one edge of the area you wish to embroider, then work straight stitches, close together, to fill in the area. **(E)**

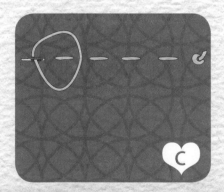
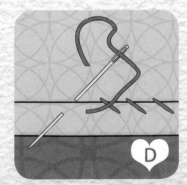
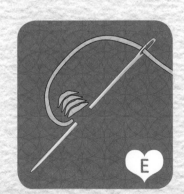

Appliqué

A little fabric cutout is one of the easiest and quickest ways to add a decorative detail, especially if the fabric used does not fray. Simply pin the cutout to the item to be decorated (or, if it is a very small piece, simply hold it in place with the thumb of your left hand as you sew) and slipstitch the edges of the motif to the background fabric, using the tip of the needle to pick up a tiny piece of the background fabric and the edge of the appliqué fabric at the same time.

Blanket stitch

This has been used to neaten the edges of some of the slippers.

With the edge of the work facing away from you, work from left to right.

1 Bring the needle up at the top edge of the fabric, in through the fabric at B and back up at C, looping the tail of thread around the needle. Pull the thread taut but not too tight, as this will pucker the fabric.

2 The stitch should lie flat with the loop of thread forming a bar across the top edge. Repeat step 1 all round the fabric edge.

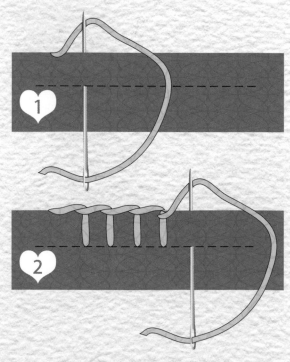

French knot

1 Bring the needle to the right side of the fabric where you want the French knot to be. Hold the thread taut with the forefinger and thumb of your left hand and use your right hand to wrap the thread around the needle tip two or three times.

2 Insert the needle tip close to the point where the thread is emerging from the fabric and pull it through to the back of the work so that the knot of yarn lies neatly on the surface of the fabric.

Chain stitch

Bring the needle up at the point you wish your row of chain stitches to begin, then reinsert it down through the same point, creating a loop of yarn or thread. Bring the needle back out through the fabric a little way along and inside the loop. Pull the yarn or embroidery thread, not too tightly, to create the first chain stitch, then reinsert the needle at the place where it last emerged and repeat to form a row of linked chain stitches. For flower petals, use a single chain stitch for each petal; this is known as 'lazy daisy' stitch.

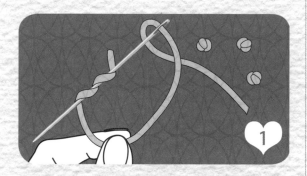

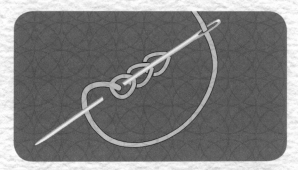

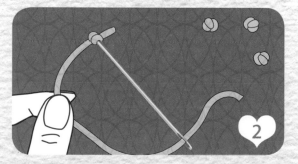

Knitting techniques

You will find these little shoes and slippers a pleasure to make; they are small and therefore quick to knit, but most involve interesting methods of construction.

Tools and materials

Using good-quality materials that are also hard-wearing is an important consideration when making knitted booties. The basic tools and equipment that you will need to tackle the knitted projects in this book are outlined below.

Yarns

The projects in this book have been made using a variety of knitting yarns of different weights, thicknesses and fibres. As a rule, I prefer to use natural fibres, particularly pure wool, or blends including cashmere and silk, as these are soft against a baby's skin. These yarns tend to be more expensive, but you will need such small quantities that it is not really so extravagant. Check the washing instructions on the ball band when buying yarn if you intend to machine-wash the slippers.

The pattern notes for each pair of slippers and booties state the actual yarns used, so it should be fairly easy to source these yarns. However, if a certain yarn is not available or you decide to substitute your own choice, you will definitely need to knit a tension sample (see opposite).

Needles

Only two sizes of needles have been used to make the knitted booties in this book: 3mm (UK11:US2/3) and 3.25mm (UK10:US3). These are smaller than you might expect – and certainly smaller than the needle sizes recommended on the ball bands of the various yarns – but they have been chosen in order to produce a firm, close-knit fabric that will hold its shape. You will need one pair of each size, plus two 3mm (UK11:US2/3) double-pointed knitting needles to make an i-cord.

Other equipment

❤ A row counter may be useful for keeping track of how many rows you have knitted.

❤ Rubber point protectors can be slipped on to your needle ends to prevent stitches from slipping off when you put your work down.

❤ To hold spare stitches, you will need a stitch holder – although for these small projects, an ordinary large safety pin will suffice, as there are very few stitches involved.

❤ A blunt tapestry needle is essential for sewing pieces of knitting together and for weaving in yarn ends.

❤ You will also need a sewing needle and thread for stitching buttons in place and small, sharp scissors for cutting yarn.

Other materials

You will need googly eyes for the Frog face and Rabbit ears booties and a small amount of toy stuffing for the Little duckling slippers. Some of the projects require ribbons and buttons; the amounts needed are listed under each project.

Tension (gauge)

It is important to check your tension (gauge) before you start knitting to ensure that your project ends up the right size. To check if your tension is correct, work a swatch using the specified yarn and needles, then measure it.

To knit a tension sample, cast on 40 stitches using the needle size stated in the pattern and work in stocking stitch (or the stitch stated in the pattern instructions) until your work measures about $5\frac{1}{2}$in (14cm); then cast off loosely.

Lay out the piece of knitting on a flat surface and use a ruler to count the number of stitches and rows over 4in (10cm). If you have more stitches and rows than the number stated in the pattern, this indicates that you knit more tightly than the stated tension and your finished item is likely to end up too small, so you will need to try again using a larger needle. If you have fewer stitches, you tend to knit more loosely, so try again with a smaller needle until you achieve the correct tension.

Basic knitting techniques

Simple cast-on

This is the main method used throughout the book; some knitters know it as 'two-needle' or 'chain' cast-on.

1 Make a slip knot and place it on the left-hand needle. *Insert the right-hand needle into the back of the loop, behind the left-hand needle, and wrap the yarn around it, as shown in the diagram.

2 Use the right-hand needle to pull the yarn through, creating a new stitch.

3 Transfer this stitch to the left-hand needle and repeat from * until you have the required number of stitches.

Cable cast-on

This creates a firm edge. It can be an initial cast-on or used when creating extra stitches.

1 Make a slip knot and place it on the left-hand needle. Make one stitch using the simple cast-on method. *For the next stitch, insert the needle between the two stitches on the left-hand needle.

2 Wrap the yarn round the right-hand needle and pull through, between the previous two stitches.

3 Transfer the stitch you have made to the left-hand needle and repeat from * until you have the required number.

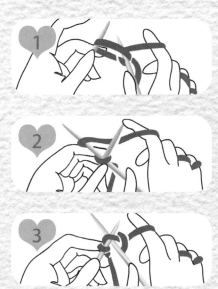

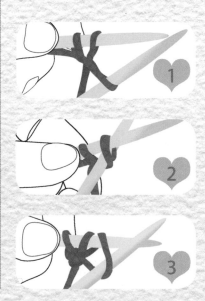

Knit stitch (k)

Rows of knit stitches produce a garter-stitch fabric; alternating rows of knit and purl stitches produce a stocking-stitch fabric. Alternating knit and purl stitches along a row produces textured effects, including rib.

1 Insert the right-hand needle into the next loop and behind the left-hand needle, then wrap the yarn around it.

2 Use the right-hand needle to pull the yarn through, creating a new stitch.

3 Keep this new stitch on the right-hand needle and continue along the row.

Purl stitch (p)

1 Begin with the yarn at the front of the work.

2 Insert the tip of the right-hand needle into the front of the next loop, in front of the left-hand needle, then wrap the yarn around it, as shown in the diagram.

3 Use the right-hand needle to pull the yarn through the first loop, creating a new stitch; keep this new stitch on the right-hand needle and continue along the row.

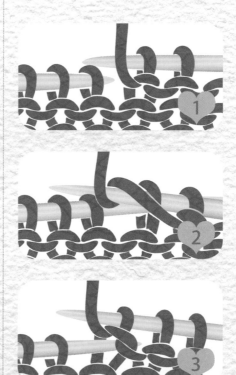

Casting off

This is usually done using knit stitches, but you may also be required to cast off in purl or rib.

1 Knit the first two stitches on to the right-hand needle; then, using the tip of the left-hand needle, slip the first stitch over the second stitch, leaving just one stitch on the needle.

2 Knit another stitch so that there are two stitches on the right-hand needle, and repeat the process until there is only one stitch left. Cut the yarn and thread the end of the yarn through the remaining stitch to fasten off.

Shaping

Each slipper or bootie is shaped to fit a baby's foot; to create the shaping, you will need to increase and decrease where the pattern instructs you to do so.

Increases are worked in one of three ways:

- by casting on extra stitches at the beginning of a row.

- by knitting into an existing stitch more than once. Where pattern states 'inc1', knit into the front and back of the stitch, thereby creating one extra stitch. Where the pattern states 'inc2', knit into the front, the back and the front again, so creating two extra stitches.

- by making an extra stitch by picking up the horizontal loop of yarn between the needles, placing it on the left-hand needle and knitting (or purling, where stated) into the back of the stitch – referred to in the pattern as M1.

Decreases are worked in a number of different ways:

- k2tog – insert the right-hand needle into the front loops of the next two stitches and knit both stitches together.

Baby Booties and Slippers

- ♥ k2tog tbl – insert the right-hand needle into the back loops of the next two stitches and knit both stitches together.

- ♥ k1, sl1, psso – slip the next stitch on to the right-hand needle, knit the next stitch, then, using the tip of the left-hand needle, slip the slipped stitch over the knitted stitch.

- ♥ p2tog – with the yarn at the front of the work, insert the right-hand needle into the front loops of the next two stitches and purl both stitches together.

- ♥ p3tog – with the yarn at the front of the work, insert the right-hand needle into the front loops of the next three stitches and purl both stitches together.

Picking up stitches

Sometimes the instructions require you to 'pick up and knit' stitches – for example, along the front of a shoe to create the instep. Use the right-hand needle to pick up a loop of yarn between stitches, wrap the yarn around it, and use the right-hand needle to pull the yarn towards you, through the loop, to create a new stitch, just as you do when knitting a row of stitches. Pick up the next loop of yarn and repeat the process until you have picked up the required number of stitches.

Making up

When working on such a small scale, the objective is to be as neat as possible. When joining the sides of two knitted pieces it is advisable to use one of two methods: mattress stitch or backstitch. When joining two straight edges – for example, on the centre of a sole – graft or oversew the edges for a neat result.

Mattress-stitch seam

This method creates an invisible seam. Thread a blunt needle with matching yarn. With the right side of the work facing, starting at the bottom edge of the work, insert the needle under the bar between the first and second stitches on the right-hand side. Insert the needle in the same way on the opposite side. Repeat, working across from left to right and back again, moving up the seam. Do not pull too tightly or you will cause the seam to pucker.

Backstitch seam

1 Thread a blunt needle with a long length of matching yarn. Place the two pieces to be joined on top of one another, right sides together.

2 Working from right to left, one stitch in from the selvedge, bring the needle up through both layers, then back down through both layers one row to the left.

3 Bring the needle back up through both layers one row to the left, then back down one row to the right, in the same place as before.

4 Repeat, taking the needle two rows to the left each time, and one row back. **(A)**

Grafting

With right sides facing and the edges placed together, insert the needle under a single stitch on one side, then under the corresponding stitch on the other side; continue in this way, zigzagging back and forth, then pull up the yarn to close the seam (do not pull too tightly, or the seam will pucker). **(B)**

Oversewing

Line up the edges to be joined and whipstitch together on the right side of the work. **(C)**

144

Making an i-cord

The i-cord is a knitted cord that can be made up of two or more stitches. In this book, several of the projects feature i-cords; for example, it is used to go through the eyelets of the Elfin boots and to thread through the top edge of the Frog face slippers (see pages 41 and 93).

Using two double-pointed needles, cast on the required number of stitches (this example shows a 5-stitch cord) and knit all stitches. Do not turn the work but slide the stitches to the opposite end of the right-hand needle, transfer this needle to the other hand and, taking the yarn firmly across the back of the work, knit the stitches. Repeat the process until the cord is the desired length. **(D)**

E

Fastenings

If you are using buttons, make sure they are stitched on securely and cannot be pulled off. Ribbons and cords are a good choice as they can be adjusted. Snap fasteners (poppers), like buttons, must be stitched securely. Another option is to use snap fasteners that are attached using a special tool that fixes them very firmly to the fabric; these can be used for knitted, crocheted or fabric shoes. Follow the manufacturer's instructions carefully to ensure that the snap fasteners are securely fixed to the fabric. **(E)**

D

Crochet techniques

Crocheting baby slippers and booties is easy and the results are charming. Crochet is very versatile, which means that most of the projects can be made in one piece, without too many seams and with very little finishing off to do.

Tools and materials

As with the sewing and knitting projects in this book, the crochet projects do not require much in the way of tools, but it is advisable to choose good-quality materials for the booties and slippers.

Yarns

The projects in this book have been made using a variety of yarns: wool and wool blend yarns produce a soft, supple fabric, while cotton yarns are crisp, easy to work with, and perfect for summer shoes to wear in the pram or pushchair. I prefer to use natural fibres, as these are soft against a baby's skin. Natural yarns tend to be a little more expensive than those composed from synthetic fibres, but you will only need small quantities, which makes them more affordable. Check the ball band when buying yarn to see if it is machine-washable.

If the specified yarn for any of the patterns is not available, or you decide to substitute another yarn, check the tension (see opposite) before proceeding with the pattern.

Hooks

Five different hook sizes have been used to make the crocheted booties and slippers: 2.50mm (UK12:USB-1/C-2), 3.00mm (UK11:USC-2/D-3), 3.50mm (UK9:USE-4), 3.75mm (UK–:USF-5) and 4.00mm (UK8:USG-6). They have been chosen to produce a particular result, and so that the finished shoes or slippers will be the correct size. Once again, it is important to check your tension so that you don't end up with slippers that are too big or too small.

Other materials

Some of the projects require ribbons and buttons; the amounts needed are listed under each project.

Other equipment

- ♥ A row counter may be useful for keeping track of how many rows you have worked, while stitch markers are handy to mark certain points in the pattern.

- ♥ A blunt tapestry needle is useful for darning in yarn ends and for sewing any seams or joining components.

- ♥ You will need a sewing needle and thread for stitching buttons in place. A small pair of scissors will be necessary for cutting yarn.

Following patterns

Before you embark on any project, make sure you have all the tools and materials you require, then read through the pattern from beginning to end to make sure you understand it.

Tension (gauge)

Check your tension (gauge) before you start crocheting your booties or slippers to make sure they end up the right size. To check that your tension is correct, work a swatch using the specified yarn and hook, then measure it using a ruler (rather than a tape measure) to count the number of stitches and rows over 4in (10cm). If you have more stitches and rows than the number stated in the pattern, this indicates that you crochet more tightly than the stated tension; your finished item is likely to end up too small, so you will have to try again using a larger hook. If you have fewer stitches, you tend to crochet more loosely, so try again with a smaller hook until you achieve the correct tension.

Basic crochet techniques

Chain stitch (ch)

1 Make a slip knot and place it on the hook. With the hook in your right hand and the yarn held in the left hand with your left forefinger controlling the tension, pull the yarn taut. Take the hook under then over the yarn.

2 Use the hook to pull the loop of yarn through the slip knot, then repeat the process, pulling the yarn through the loop on the hook, to form a foundation chain.

Slip stitch (sl st)

1 Push the crochet hook into the top of the next stitch (or through the top of the chain loop when working along the foundation chain), and wrap the yarn around the hook.

2 Use the hook to draw the yarn back through both the top of the stitch and the loop on the hook.

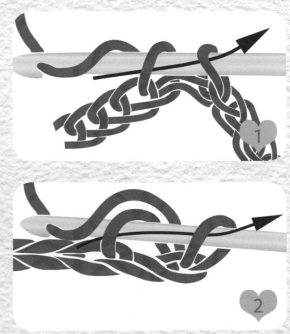

Double crochet (dc)

1 Insert the hook into the next stitch, wrap the yarn over the hook and draw the yarn through to the front.

2 Wrap the yarn around the hook again and draw it through both loops on the hook.

Half treble (htr)

1 Yarn over the hook, then insert the hook into the next stitch. Yarn over and draw the loop through to the front.

2 Yarn over the hook and draw through all three loops on the hook.

Crochet techniques

Treble (tr)

1 Yarn over the hook, then insert the hook into the next stitch.

2 Yarn over the hook and draw the loop through to the front.

3 Yarn over the hook and draw through the first two loops on the hook.

4 Yarn over again and draw through the remaining two loops on the hook.

Double treble (dtr)

1 Yarn over the hook twice, then insert the hook into the next stitch.

2 Yarn over the hook and draw the loop through to the front.

3 Yarn over the hook and draw through the first two loops on the hook.

4 Yarn over the hook and draw through the next two loops on the hook.

5 Yarn over again and draw through the remaining two loops on the hook.

Baby Booties and Slippers

Foundation chain

To make a flat fabric worked in rows, you must start with a foundation chain. Make a slip knot, then work the number of chains stated in the pattern. When working in the round, the foundation chain is usually joined to create a ring into which you work the first round of stitches.

Magic loop

Instead of beginning with a ring of foundation chains, you can make a loop using the tail of yarn. Crochet the first round of stitches into this, then pull the yarn tail to close the centre up tight.

Working in rows or rounds

To produce a flat crocheted fabric, stitches are worked into the foundation chain, then into the tops of stitches on subsequent rows, turning the work at the end of each row. One or more chains are worked at the beginning of each row in place of the first stitch. When working in rounds, the work is not usually turned (unless stated in the pattern instructions).

Shaping

Each slipper or bootie is shaped to fit a baby's foot; to create the shaping you will need to increase and decrease where the pattern instructs you to do so.

Increases are generally achieved by working two or more stitches into one stitch. Decreasing is usually done by working two or more stitches together or by missing a stitch and working into the next one. Follow the pattern instructions carefully; they will tell you when and how to increase and decrease.

Making up

Most crocheted pieces can be joined by oversewing. On some of the projects in this book, pieces are joined by slipstitching edges together, or by working a row of double crochet into both edges at once – for example, when joining a sole and an upper.

Add-on soles

Soles cut from fabric, leather or non-slip material can be stitched on top of the knitted or crocheted ones. For the sewn projects, you could substitute leather or non-slip soles for the fabric ones.

Adding leather soles

Leather soles create a firm base, make slippers and booties more hard-wearing, and give a degree of grip – but can still be slippery on polished surfaces. Choose a soft leather and cut out sole shapes using the template on page 155.

There is no need to hem leather as it does not fray but for sewing you will need to use a special leather needle, which has a sharp, triangular tip that cuts through the leather. Simply oversew the edges of the sole to the base of your slipper or bootie.

Non-slip soles

Remember that slippers and booties made from fabric and yarn are not intended for walking. Just like socks, they offer no support and the soles are slippery, especially on hard floors. To create a non-slip sole, you will need to cut out a sole shape from non-slip fabric and stitch this to the base of each slipper or bootie. Non-slip fabrics can be purchased from hardware shops, where they are sold for applying to the underside of table mats and rugs to prevent them from sliding around. Another method is to use a rubber solution specially designed for applying to knitted or crocheted socks and slippers to make them non-slip.

Adding velvet soles

Needlecord or suedette would also make good fabrics for this purpose.

1 Use two pieces of velvet, each at least 8 x 12in (20 x 30cm), and transfer the sole pattern (on page 155) in the desired size twice on to the wrong side of one of the pieces. Place them right sides together, and stitch through both layers, following the lines and leaving a gap of about 1¼–1½in (3–4cm) on one of the straight sides of each sole.

2 Cut out the shapes, adding a ¼in (6mm) seam allowance all round.

3 Turn each sole right sides out, tuck in the seam allowance on the open edge, and slipstitch the folded edges together to close the gap.

4 Slipstitch the edge of each sole to the outer edge at the base of each bootie.

Baby shoe sizes

This chart is intended as a guide to help you decide which size to make for your baby. Just using your baby's age as a guide may not be accurate as he or she may have larger or smaller feet than average. To make sure the slippers or booties fit, with wriggle room for little toes, you should measure the length of your baby's feet, using a tape measure or place them on the template outline opposite and make the size indicated on the chart.

UK size	Euro size	US size	approx. age	length (cm)	length (in)
0	16	1	0–3 months	9.5cm	$3\frac{3}{4}$in
1	17	2	3–6 months	10cm	4in
2	18	3	6–9 months	11.5cm	$4\frac{1}{2}$in
3	19	4	9–12 months	12.5cm	$4\frac{7}{8}$in
4	20	5	12–15 months	13cm	5in
5	22	6	15–18 months	14cm	$5\frac{1}{2}$in
6	23	7	18–24 months	15cm	6in
7	24	8	24–36 months	16cm	$6\frac{1}{4}$in

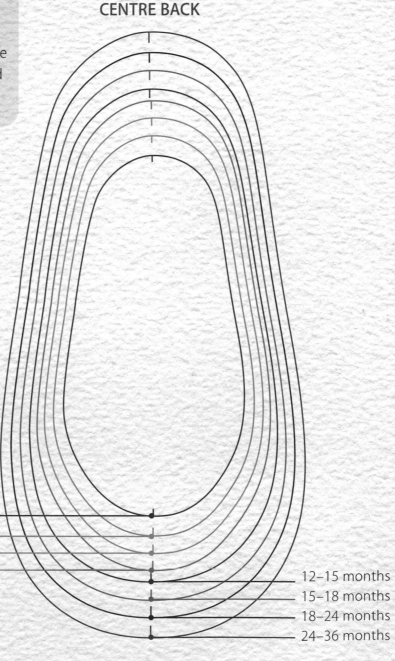

Add-on soles

You can also use these template outlines to make add-on soles as explained on pages 152–3.

CENTRE BACK

0–3 months
3–6 months
6–9 months
9–12 months

12–15 months
15–18 months
18–24 months
24–36 months

CENTRE FRONT

Abbreviations

Knitting abbreviations

beg	begin(ning)
cm	centimetre(s)
dec	decrease
inc	increase
in	inch(es)
inc1	knit into front and back of same stitch
inc2	knit into front, back and front of stitch
k	knit
k2tog	knit 2 together (decrease by 1 stitch)
k2tog tbl	knit 2 together through back loops (decrease by 1 stitch)
m1	make a stitch by picking up the loop between stitches and knitting (or purling) into the back of it
mm	millimetre(s)
p	purl
p2tog	purl 2 together (decrease by 1 stitch)
p3tog	purl 2 together (decrease by 2 stitches)
p2tog tbl	purl 2 together through back loops (decrease by 1 stitch)
psso	pass the slipped stitch over
rem	remaining
rep	repeat
RS	right side
sl	slip
st(s)	stitch(es)
st st	stocking stitch
tbl	through back loop(s)
WS	wrong side
yfwd	yarn forward

*	work instructions immediately following *, then repeat as directed
( )	repeat instructions inside brackets as many times as instructed

Crochet abbreviations

beg	begin(ning)
ch	chain
ch sp	chain space
cm	centimetre(s)
dc	double crochet (US: single crochet)
dc2tog	work 2 double crochet together over next two stitches (decrease by 1 stitch)
dtr	double treble (US: triple)
htr	half treble (US: half double crochet)
htr4tog	work 4 half treble together over next four stitches (decrease by 3 stitches)
in	inch(es)
mm	millimetre(s)
rep	repeat
RS	right side
sl st	slip stitch
sp	space
st	stitch
tr	treble (US: double crochet)
WS	wrong side
*	work instructions immediately following *, then repeat as directed
( )	repeat instructions inside brackets as many times as instructed

Conversions

Knitting needles

UK	Metric	US
14	2mm	0
13	2.25mm	1
12	2.75mm	2
11	3mm	–
10	3.25mm	3
–	3.5mm	4
9	3.75mm	5
8	4mm	6
7	4.5mm	7
6	5mm	8
5	5.5mm	9
4	6mm	10
3	6.5mm	10.5
2	7mm	10.5
1	7.5mm	11
0	8mm	13
000	10mm	15

Crochet hooks

UK	Metric	US
14	2.00mm	–
13	2.25mm	B-1
12	2.50mm	–
–	2.75mm	C-2
11	3.00mm	–
10	3.25mm	D-3
9	3.50mm	E-4
–	3.75mm	F-5
8	4.00mm	G-6
7	4.50mm	7
6	5.00mm	H-8
5	5.50mm	I-9
4	6.00mm	J-10
3	6.50mm	K-10.5
2	7.00mm	–
0	8.00mm	L-11
00	9.00mm	M–N-13
000	10.00mm	N–P-15

UK/US crochet terms

UK	US
Double crochet	Single crochet
Half treble	Half double crochet
Treble	Double crochet
Double treble	Triple crochet
Treble treble	Double triple crochet

UK/US yarn weights

UK	US
2-ply	Lace
3-ply	Fingering
4-ply	Sport
DK (double knitting)	Light worsted
Aran	Fisherman/ worsted
Chunky	Bulky
Super chunky	Extra bulky

About the author

Having studied Fine Art at the Slade School, Susie Johns began her publishing career as a magazine and partworks editor before becoming a freelance writer and designer. She is the author of more than thirty craft books, on a range of subjects including knitting, crochet, papier mâché and collage. She has also contributed to a number of magazines, such as *Let's Knit*, *Crafts Beautiful*, *Embroidery*, *Needlecraft*, *Woman's Weekly*, *Family Circle*, *Practical Parenting* and *Art Attack* and has made several television appearances demonstrating various crafts. She particularly enjoys art and craft activities that involve recycling and reinventing. Susie is a qualified teacher and runs workshops in drawing and painting, knitting and crochet, embroidery, and 3D Design. Her previous books for GMC Publications include *Knitted Finger Puppets* and *Knitted Pets*.

Acknowledgements

Thanks to Coats Patons, Rowan, Sirdar, Artesano and Designer Yarns for supplying most of the yarns used throughout this book. A big 'thank you' to Gerrie Purcell for asking me to do the book in the first place, to Virginia Brehaut for managing the project so patiently, and to Marilyn Wilson and Penny Hill for meticulous pattern-checking. I should also like to add a long-lasting 'thank you' to my children for their invaluable patience, support and feedback.

Index

add-on soles 152–153, 155
appliqué 136

backstitch seams 135, 144
basting 134
bias bindings 36
blanket stitch 136

cable cast-on 140
casting off 142
chain stitch 137
chain stitch (ch) 148
crochet hooks 146–147, 157
crochet techniques 146–151

double crochet (dc) 149, 157
double treble (dtr) 150, 157

embellishments 133
equipment 133, 138–139,
    146–147

fabric types 132
fastenings 145
foundation chain 151
French knots 137

gauge 139, 147

grafting 144

half treble (htr) 149, 157
hand stitches 135–137
hooks 146–147, 157

i-cords 145

knit stitch (k) 141
knitting needles 138, 157
knitting techniques 138–145

lace 133
leather 64, 152

magic loop 151
making up 143–145, 151
mattress-stitch seams 143

needles 133, 138, 157
non-slip soles 8, 152, 153

oversewing 144

pattern pieces 134
picking up stitches 143
pre-shrinking 12, 132
purl stitch (p) 141

ribbon 133
rounds 151
rows 151
running stitch 135

safety 8, 16, 112, 133, 153
satin stitch 135
seams 134, 143
sewing techniques 134–137
shaping 142–143, 151
shoe sizes 154–155
shrinkage 12, 132
simple cast-on 140
sizing 154–155
slip stitch (sl st) 148
slipstitch (sewing) 135
soles 8, 73, 152–153, 155

tacking 134
tension (gauge) 139, 147
thread 132–133
tools 133, 138–139, 146–147
treble (tr) 150, 157

velvet soles 153

yarns 138, 146, 157

To place an order, or to request a catalogue, contact:

GMC Publications Ltd

Castle Place, 166 High Street, Lewes, East Sussex,

BN7 1XU, United Kingdom

Tel: 01273 488005

www.gmcbooks.com